MARRIAGE CHALLENGES
LEAVING A LEGACY OF LOVE

FABYONNE WILLIAMS

Marriage Challenges
by Fabyonne Williams
Copyright ©2016 Fabyonne Williams

All rights reserved. This book is protected under the copyright laws of the United States of America. This book may not be copied or reprinted for commercial gain or profit.

ISBN 978-1-63360-040-9
For Worldwide Distribution

Printed in the U.S.A.

This book is dedicated to my wonderful, loving husband Sheldon, who has always been in my corner. He has prayed me through the rough times and encouraged me when I needed it most. He also accompanies me on this emotional roller coaster of a relationship ride that I wouldn't trade for the world. Without our very wild and crazy marriage, I would have no expertise in this area, so for that I am forever grateful.

I would also like to acknowledge my pastor, Dr. Rockwell Dillaman, and his lovely wife, Karen. I refer to his sermons, nuggets of knowledge, and funny quips numerous times. He has taught me to express my love for God by showing love to His people. He and his wife are also one of our marriage mentor couples, and their over forty years of marriage are a testament to the power of putting God first in your relationship.

Words of appreciation for *Marriage Challenges*

"It has been my privilege to pastor and subsequently minister alongside Sheldon and Fabyonne Williams. My wife and I count them among our dearest friends. Their compassion and commitment toward those who struggle in marriage are clearly born of the Holy Spirit. Their humility and transparency where their own "intense fellowship" is concerned are refreshing. You will see that for yourself in these pages! Knowing their personal lives and their commitment, I highly recommend this book as a resource.

My mother often echoed the quote, 'If wishes were horses, beggars would ride!', and with good cause. Far too often, people fail in their marriage because they substitute the sedative of wishful thinking for the stimulant of action. This book can serve as an antidote to that practice. It offers action steps that lead to discovery and renewal." - **Dr. Rockwell Dillaman, Lead Pastor, Allegheny Center Alliance Church**

"Fabyonne writes with the authenticity of experience. Her book is a compilation of not just challenges she's set up for couples like us, but real-life challenges she's encountered with her husband. We love this book because it feels like we are sitting down with a cup of coffee and talking about marriage with Fabyonne. Her advice and adventures are worth taking!" - **Hilary and Marv Nelson, author of *What Good is Jesus?***

"God has given the Williams a gift to help heal and restore marriages in a time when marriage is increasingly devalued. *Marriage Challenges: Leaving a Legacy of Love* is a good read for anyone who looks to strengthen his or her marriage. In this book, Fabyonne guides couples through date-night ideas, challenging games and exercises, devotions, and prayers. The challenges in the book are not only great conversation starters, they are also a lot of fun, and would also be useful for marriage retreats. This is an exceptional book!" - **Dr. Arthur & Charlene Woods**

TABLE OF CONTENTS

Foreword — vii
Introduction — ix

week 1 Marriage Resolution — 1
week 2 80/20 Rule — 5
week 3 The 10 Commandments (Marriage Version) — 8
week 4 The 10 Commandments (Marriage Version) Part 2 — 11
week 5 "I Didn't Think It Was Cheating." — 14
week 6 Each One Teach One — 17
week 7 This Too Shall Pass — 19
week 8 Money, Money, Money, Money, Money — 21
week 9 Our Money Plan — 24
week 10 The Marriage I Want, Not the Marriage I Have — 26
week 11 20 Questions Marriage Version — 28
week 12 Life's Too Short — 31
week 13 Let's Talk About Sex — 34
week 14 Mission Possible (Love Letters) — 36
week 15 God First — 38
week 16 Burn, Baby, Burn — 41
week 17 Love is Patient, Love is Kind — 43
week 18 Just for the Health of It — 46
week 19 I Should Have Bought You Flowers — 48
week 20 Accountability — 51
week 21 I Want a Divorce — 55
week 22 Make Me Laugh — 57
week 23 Love in the New Year — 59
week 24 Seen and Not Heard — 62
week 25 Secrets — 64
week 26 The FOO Fighters — 66
week 27 Love Hurts — 69
week 28 Marriage Can be Messy — 72

week 29 Make it Last Forever	75
week 30 People Watching	79
week 31 Happy Divorce-iversary	81
week 32 Speaking the Language of Love	84
week 33 A Prayer for My Husband	87
week 34 "I Don't Even Like Talking to You."	89
week 35 A Fair One	92
week 36 Dating Ideas for Couples	95
week 37 Make Me Happy	97
week 38 Sticks and Stones	100
week 39 Loose Lips Sink Ships - and Marriages	103
week 40 Yours, Mine and Ours	106
week 41 Sex Starts in the Kitchen	110
week 42 Sex Starts in the Kitchen - Part 2	113
week 43 The Power of Porn	117
week 44 Taking One for the Team	122
week 45 I Love You, but I Don't Like You	125
week 46 Affair-Proof Your Marriage	129
week 47 Make Marriage Fun	134
week 48 In Sickness and in Health	137
week 49 Marriage Revival	140
week 50 Happy Husband's Day	143
week 51 Temptation	145
week 52 She Really Loves Him	148
Prologue	151
Appendix One: Encouraging Bible Passages	153
Appendix Two: Month-by-Month Dating Ideas	155
Appendix Three: Budget Spreadsheet	165
Appendix Four: The Feeling Wheel	176

FOREWORD
BY KAREN DILLAMAN

This foreword started out as an endorsement for Fabyonne's book, which, by the way, I think is a wonderful effort that will help many people. My husband and I are honored to be a part of this book, for we are the anonymous cruising couple married 42 years to whom Fabyonne refers in Week 16.

Fortunately for all of us, Fabyonne lets us know in Week 10 she is writing about the marriage she wants to have, not the one she has. In Week 10, she informed us she and Sheldon do not wear wonderful matching pajamas to bed. What a relief! Without that admission, I would have wondered about the true condition of my marriage, despite our longevity. Frankly, I would have been jealous if they had!

As I read the manuscript, I found a statement in Week 21 to be the key for all the challenges Fabyonne presents. There she wrote, "Grass is only greener where you water it." Having written that, she goes on to provide married couples with a gushing hose. Our marriages will be great only if we work on them, and Fabyonne has given us so many ideas, it would be impossible to fail.

As you read, notice how many times prayer is mentioned.

I can't imagine a woman reading this book a week at a time. I would want to see what I was getting into before ever starting. Fabyonne's easy flow and sense of humor make you want to read on—at least for me. She has made herself vulnerable and has shared some intimate insights into her own marriage with brutal and humorous honesty.

Blessed is the husband who would actually be willing to work on this 52-week challenge. I could see a wife reading this and not telling her husband where she was getting all the wonderful challenges for them to work on, acting like she thought them up herself. When we as wives begin to do what's in this book, our husbands will respond.

I can't wait to get some copies of this book in my hands so I can give them to people I know. Sheldon and Fabyonne have been instrumental in helping so many married couples in our church. Even with 42 years under my belt, I was convicted and reminded over and over again about what I could do to improve my marriage.

Thank you, Fabyonne, for your commitment to seeing our marriages be all they can be, all that God intended them to be. I would write more, but I am already considering how to incorporate a few of the challenges in our marriage now that I am retired. I will fill you in on how they went.

Karen Dillaman
September, 2016

INTRODUCTION

As I write this book, my husband Sheldon and I have been married for 21 years, and we are both aspiring marriage and family therapists. We have three wonderful adult children, a daughter-in-love (I never did like the term daughter-in-law, so since we love her, we changed the term), and four absolutely perfect grandchildren with one more on the way. We have been counseling couples as lay counselors in our church for the past 15 years. That role began as a matter of happenstance, but we have found a love in working with couples that exceeded the love for our careers.

The churches we have attended usually sponsored wonderful premarital sessions and great after-divorce support groups. My husband describes those ministries as the book ends. We saw it as a problem that there was nothing in between those groups for married couples. It was as if churches believed that couples were well prepared for marriage, and there was no need to sponsor any type of ministry for them. Once people were married, they had each other, so it was unnecessary to have something specifically geared toward couples. We did not find this to be the case.

You have heard the saying that "it takes a village to raise a child." We believe the same to be true for marriage. Younger couples need to see healthy, older couples who are thriving in their relationships, couples who have been working at marriage longer than others and who have survived many trials and tribulations. Then we saw that all couples need to see peer couples who are working through similar issues so they have someone with whom they can identify. When one hears another couple talk about their struggles, that couple can be surprised and say, "You too? We are facing the same thing!" Every couple also needs to give something back to the village by mentoring a younger couple and encouraging them to stay the course. You would be surprised how much people glean from just being around a couple that shows love to one another while walking out daily activities. This is also part of that legacy of love I so often stress.

We did not see this happening in our church, so Shel and I started small with something we called "The Marriage Fellowship." This was a monthly event where any Christian married couple was welcome. We limited it to believers because it originated in our church and everything was based on biblical precepts. We held it in our home and would spend the evening with other couples praying, talking, laughing, and even crying about marriage. Couples who attended began to trust and confide in us. They would come to find a listening ear, a shoulder to cry on, and someone to encourage them that they can make it. From that start, the rest, as they say, is history.

We decided to return to school for another Master's Degree when the couples we were counseling would sometimes divorce or separate. This was devastating, and we would mourn and wonder if we had done enough. We found ourselves at the end of our level of expertise, but knew we loved working with couples. Although going to school together was challenging and put tremendous stress on our own marriage, it was one of the best decisions we have ever made. We struggled through the hard stuff and celebrated the good together. It strengthened our bond and understanding for one another. It also helped us to be more compassionate toward other couples as we experienced the rough patches we went through.

What does all of that have to do with this book? Everything and nothing at all (I absolutely love saying that, it just sounds so puzzling and intriguing). The book was born out of that marital support group, a struggling blog, and a few of what we termed "Facebook Challenges" that we sponsored for couples. Facebook was inundated over the last few years with challenges, and I admit that I was drawn into accepting some of them like, "The Five-Day-Ab Challenge," "The Squat Challenge," and "The Ten-Day Smoothie Challenge," just to name a few. It gave us the idea to have a Marriage Challenge, or as we termed it, The Seven-Day Love Challenge.

Couples competed to complete all of the challenges in a seven-day period. They had to complete the challenge, take pictures and record a video of themselves completing the challenges, which they then had to post to a closed Facebook group within a designated time frame. Some of the challenges were silly and others got quite serious. The couples could go from running through a park kissing statues to reading the Song of Solomon together and attempting to interpret its meaning. From the fifty couples who participated, winners emerged or ties were broken with an exhausting tiebreaker. While the couples were caught up in the spirit of competition, God was working miraculously in their relationships.

When we began to get sincere comments about how the challenges restored broken marriages, healed areas of pain, or allowed children to watch their parents fall in love again, we knew this had to become bigger and go farther. There had to be a way to touch more couples, and our hope and prayer is that this book is one such vehicle. We have one request: When you see the blessing in this for your marriage, pay it forward by recommending or even gifting a copy to another couple. You can be an integral part of what God is doing on behalf of marriages everywhere by taking that simple step.

This book is different than a page-by-page couple's guide to marriage. This is set up in a devotional format, but it's not a Bible study. The plan is for you to take an entire week to work through each entry for the next year (yes, I said year). You will need to dig deep in order to maintain your healthy marriage or to restore your struggling relationship back to health. This will be challenging, but you can do it. Think of this book as a marriage retreat that you can do together, in your home, with little or no expense. The ultimate purpose is to strengthen your marital bond, which in turn allows the two of you to leave a legacy of love for everyone your relationship touches.

There is no particular strategy to how the weeks are arranged, but I recommend you address them in the order they are presented. You will have an assignment each week, along with a verse or passage from the Bible on which to meditate and focus. Some weeks will be more directed toward the husband or wife, but each week has something for you to do as a couple. You will discover as you read and apply the principles that I love lists! What better way to prepare you for the journey ahead, therefore, than to give you a *list* of things you can do to prepare for and work your way through this 52-week marriage retreat.

1. Pray. Pray for your marriage that it will grow and not be stifled by the challenges ahead. Pray that God will bless your efforts and help you to build every area of your relationship. Take time to pray for the others who are taking on the challenge so that God can help them increase their time together and to improve their marital bond. Satan, our great enemy, recognizes the strength in your union and that is why he works so hard to destroy it. The Word tells us, "Where two or three gather in my name, there am I with them" (Matthew 18:20 NIV). Therefore, pray together and make His presence the most important part of your journey.

2. Schedule. Plan how the two of you will complete the challenge together. The challenge will require you to set aside time to work through the activities for the week and then to come together and discuss what you've learned. Pull out your calendars and pencil one another in. Better yet, write it in ink and make this an untouchable, intentional time together. If your weekends are slower, set aside an evening on the weekend to talk about what you read and how well you implemented the activity. Be sure to develop a backup plan in case you get out of rhythm due to some family or work crisis. For example, if one of you has a business trip, do not skip that week. Instead, have a backup plan in place. This backup plan could include prayer time via Skype or Tango, or an intentional discussion in a particular time slot. It may push you back a week, but you have a lifetime to work on the principles in this book that you will study over the next year.

    3. Be present. This is not the time to meet armed with your iPad, computer, and smartphone. I'm guilty of multi-tasking by checking papers (I was a school teacher), checking Facebook on my phone or email on my laptop, all while "listening" to my husband. If possible, make this a technology-free time. If the children are distracting you, use this year to create a bedtime norm for them, preferably as early as possible. Then use the quiet time to work on your marriage. Be completely present for one another. Look one another in the eye when you talk. Try some mirroring and clarification techniques. After your spouse says something important, respond with, "What I hear you saying is…" and allow him or her to clarify what you said if need be.

    4. Be intimate. I have heard intimacy described as Into-Me-See. In order to improve your relationship, you have to make it a goal to be as intimate and transparent as possible. Sex is the prescribed method of intimacy, but that's simply not realistic for 365 days. With that in mind, make it your goal to be intimate at least once a week. I realize this may take some time and scheduling, but whatever it takes, be intimate every single week while you are walking through the book.

    5. Don't give up. If you get upset as you work through this program, take a timeout, shake it off, and pick back up where you left off. A timeout looks different for everyone, so do not force how you do your timeout on your spouse. I also caution against taking too much time to get yourself together. Apply this guideline: If it takes more than a week to get back in the game, you may need the help of an impartial third party, or a licensed listener. The longer it takes you to shake off the upset, the more opportunity the enemy has to drive a wedge between the two of you, and we can't have that. If you fall behind a week, don't fret. Just pick up the next week right where you left off.

6. Create a fuss-free zone. When you enter into challenge time (however that looks for you), suspend all arguments and disagreements, or the desire to be snarky. If you can't be nice, "fake it till you make it." Many times you'll find yourself laughing or crying together and will forget about the argument because your love quota is being filled. So don't sweat the small stuff, especially during your challenge time.

7. Use a journal. The problem with taking mental notes is that the ink fades too quickly. Don't rely on your memory to retain the lessons you learn. Write them down and review them throughout the year so you can track your progress and be encouraged.

If your schedule or situation is unique, make up your own rules for how you will complete this 52-week course. Discover what works best for you and stick to it. No one is grading you, so please do not grade or evaluate one another. This is your marriage retreat done your way. The intentional quality time will build your marital bond; the activities and scriptural references will simply enhance that.

There you have the rules of engagement for the next 52 weeks. Shel and I pray that God will be with you every week when you meet, and every day when you work on your assignments. If we can help you, our contact information is at the end of the book, after the Appendix, which includes a month-by-month idea guide for your weekly dates! Now, I invite you to enter into these 52 love challenges that will help you establish a legacy of love and intimacy that will bless your family for generations to come.

Fabyonne Williams
Pittsburgh, PA
September, 2016

WEEK ONE
MARRIAGE RESOLUTION

When a new year begins, many people make resolutions; you probably do this as well. People resolve to lose weight, get a new job, read the Bible more, and some even make resolutions not to make any resolutions! Included in your resolutions every year (hoping you did not resolve to make no resolutions), I suggest you come up with a marriage resolution. The most difficult task in the world is making two become one, and becoming one is a constant work in progress. Therefore, at least once a year, reevaluate the way you are living out your vows together. Doing that may help make this process a bit easier.

Remember, there is no wrong time to make a resolution. Whenever you pick up this book and start the 52-week journey, I implore the two of you to make some type of marriage resolution concerning the progress you would like to make in the next 12 months,

Here are just a few ideas for your marriage resolution.

1. *I resolve to be the best husband/wife to my spouse this year.* This must be according to their definition of what "best" means for them. This means getting to know your spouse's likes, dislikes, wants, and needs.

2. *I resolve to make my spouse smile as many times as possible in the coming year.* Take some time each day to laugh together. Whatever it takes, do something silly, funny, or out of the ordinary to make your relationship happy and healthy.

3. *I resolve to spend as much quality time as I can with my spouse in the next 12 months.* This includes going out to eat or to concerts, as well as quiet time at home. Make this a priority. Set aside time and days of the week and mark them on your calendar as being untouchable.

4. *I resolve to perform as many PDAs (public displays of affection) as we can muster in the next year. This can also be stated as I resolve to make young people sick as they watch us openly express our love for one another.* Make your love public. Although the description above is somewhat silly, it is quite important. There's no need to go completely out of character and get out of line, but public touching, holding hands, and kissing help to strengthen your bond. It can also act as great payback to an unruly teenager, and it serves two purposes: 1) It embarrasses them, which is something every good parent must do at some point in their child's life; 2) It solidifies as a memory and seals that legacy of love in their mind.

5. *I resolve to discover more of my spouse's favorite things and then provide my partner with as many as possible in the next year.* This doesn't have to be the Porsche he's always wanted, but it could be going to his favorite action movie. It could be a box of chocolates (preferably the Sarris' nut assortment if Sheldon happens to be reading) that's just too expensive for her to buy for herself.

6. *I resolve to listen to my spouse.* You will listen when he has a bad day or when her day was phenomenal. You will work to empathize with his pain and sorrow, or to listen to all of her dreams and aspirations. God gave us two ears and one mouth for a reason – you should listen twice as much as you talk. People pay counselors lots of money just to listen. Why not save some money and listen to one another's every whim? Don't judge, just listen.

I must add a disclaimer here: There is absolutely nothing

wrong with hiring a licensed listener. I actually recommend counseling for everyone, especially married couples because, as was stated before, making two become one is quite difficult. The point here is that sometimes counseling is unnecessary when spouses have a listening ear at home.

7. *I resolve to love my spouse through thick and thin, in good times and in bad.* This one is somewhat self-explanatory. Wedding vows include the words, "for richer or poorer and in sickness and in health," purposely recognizing the importance of loving no matter what the situation. This one is simply putting those vows into practice.

8. *I resolve to pray for my spouse daily.* You should pray for every aspect of your life together, and your life as individuals outside of your marriage (careers, ministries, civic involvement). Pray for your marriage, your children and grandchildren, your plans and everything you endeavor to do. Pray for his (and her) hopes and dreams to be fulfilled and that God will bless your union.

THE CHALLENGE

If you are anything like me, you skipped over the Introduction and went right to Week One. The challenge for today is to return to the Introduction. There I included a list of things to do to prepare for this book. Take the time to do all of those things, which include, but are not limited to:

- Pray.
- Schedule time together.
- Be present.
- Be intimate.
- Don't give up.
- Create a fuss-free zone.
- Use a journal.

I won't repeat everything here, but I will add that it is vital to pray for the year ahead because you have taken on a challenge to improve your marriage. For that reason alone, the enemy is angry and will come at you with as many weapons as he can muster. Pray a covering over your relationship and the extra time and energy you will need to work together. Schedule how you will complete your challenges. Get rid of distractions so you can be present with your spouse. Make an extra effort to be as intimate as you possibly can. Even if you falter, don't ever give up. Pick yourself up, dust yourself off, and get right back into the book. Don't allow the challenge to become an argument. Table all issues in order to complete them. Finally, purchase a journal for each of you and use it as often as possible.

Once you have all of the ground rules and materials, make a resolution for your marriage. You may want to use something from the eight suggestions above, or to come up with one of your own, but make your separate resolutions. When you have made your own, come together to talk and pray about the resolution each of you has made. This may be something you want to hang on a mirror, on the fridge, or in some prominent place that will jog your memory when the two of you are at odds.

VERSE TO REMEMBER

"Let us not become weary in doing good, for at the proper time we will reap a harvest if we do not give up" (Galatians 6:9, NIV).

WEEK TWO
80/20 RULE

Extramarital affairs are nothing new. They have destroyed the lives, families, and careers of many, yet they continue to happen. Some people live with the mindset, "It can't happen to me or us," when the complete opposite is true. The 80/20 rule addresses one of the reasons we naively fall into the trap of illicit affairs. Most people don't set out to have one; they simply fall prey to one of the enemy's most successful strategies.

Allow me to explain. The 80/20 Rule states that your spouse fulfills about 80% of your wants and needs. No one fulfills 100% because we are human – diverse, ever-changing, and always emerging from some life experience that leaves us different than ever before. Assuming the 80% is accurate, you may still long to have the other 20% met as well. Your spouse makes you happy, but you wish he would hold you in the middle of the night without sex being the goal. You wish she would listen to the events of your day without interrupting. You wish that he would post his love for you all over social media, or that she would leave you alone while you're watching the game.

Your spouse is often perfect for the wants and desires you

have. You are compatible on many levels, yet both of you were born greedy and fallible, so your focus is often on that missing 20%. The affair occurs when you find an individual who has everything your spouse does not. Sadly, it takes time to recognize you are giving up 80% for 20%. No matter how you do the math, this is a losing situation.

I first heard this Rule in a Tyler Perry movie about marriage and, after analyzing many of the couples who have sat with my husband and me after being torn apart by an affair, I find this Rule to be accurate. To avoid the 80/20 Rule ruining your relationship, develop an attitude of gratitude for all your spouse offers you. Do the difficult work of focusing on what is good about your spouse instead of focusing on the negative. Make notes in your journal if you have to, but be diligent to focus on the good in your spouse, the things you love about him or her, and the reasons you fell in love in the first place.

The most important safeguard that will keep you from falling into the 80/20 trap is to recommit your marriage to God. This means adding a time of prayer when the two of you read, discuss, or write in your journal about the Bible. Doing this together puts your household in one accord. Remember to commit yourself to God and to your spouse, and to focus on the 80% you have as opposed to the 20% you don't.

THE CHALLENGE

This week, reflect on the truth that your spouse cannot meet all your needs — only God can. Where have you placed unreasonable expectations on your spouse, thus setting you up for falling into the 80/20 Trap?

Spend the week praying about this. If you are struggling to figure out what these areas may be, ask God to reveal them to you (or your spouse because he or she can see many of your blind spots). Finally, come together to have a conversation about it. This may include praying together as well as apologizing to one another (if need be). Most importantly, resolve to create a marriage that can withstand any type of temptation.

VERSE TO REMEMBER

"You are altogether beautiful my darling; there is no flaw in you" (Song of Solomon 4:7, NIV).

WEEK THREE
THE 10 COMMANDMENTS (MARRIAGE VERSION) PART 1

The Ten Commandments are rules, principles, and laws God gave Moses to share with the Israelites to guide and shape their behavior. They reminded them how important reverence, love, and trust in God would be for their journey. In the Marriage Version, the Commandments are there so you will remember that God must remain at the center of your marriage, but also to help you maintain your respect, love, and trust in your spouse to keep your relationship intact. Let's cover the first five Commandments this week.

1. Thou shalt have no other gods before me.

In your marriage, there should be no one ranked above your spouse. He or she is the king or queen, the top of the top, and head of all. Consider your spouse first when making decisions and in all you do. Keep a picture of your spouse handy, preferably something that pulls on your heart strings and reminds you why you fell in love. Your spouse should always be number one.

2. Thou shalt not make idols.

An idol in marriage is anything that draws you away from absolute romantic devotion to your spouse. Make time for your spouse and rid yourself of things that take away from your quality time. This could be anything from a TV show to a video game, a sporting event or work that is constantly entering your home and interfering with your quality time. Those things are what I am referring to as a marriage idol. Make time with your spouse sacred and keep it a priority.

3. Thou shalt not take the name of the Lord thy God in vain.

Don't take your spouse for granted. The First Commandment was to keep your spouse on a pedestal, and when you neglect to do that, you begin to take your spouse for granted. You then lose respect for one another and resort to doing and saying things you should not say even to your worst enemy. When you forget how important your spouse is, they become another face in the crowd and this attitude drives a wedge between the two of you. Also, don't refer to your spouse when talking to others as "he" or "she" when they are standing right next to you! Forgive me for my old school upbringing coming out, but I recall my grandmother having a fit when we spoke about her (or any adult present) with pronouns. Having a cute nickname for your spouse that is just between the two of you, or a loving reference rather than a distant one, will also help you remember that your connection is special and not to be taken for granted.

4. Remember the Sabbath day, to keep it holy.

Date night must be a staple in your relationship. There must be a set apart time in each week that you devote only to your spouse. Much like that sacred time with each other that I spoke of earlier, this must be an uninterrupted time. If a sitter is not an option and the kids are old enough, let them know you are not to be disturbed unless someone is bleeding or dying. If they aren't old enough to leave you alone, put them to bed extra early. Resort to Benadryl if need be. I'm kidding about the Benadryl, but you can wake them up early that morning or skip the afternoon nap. Maintain this private time for the two of you by any means necessary!

5. Honor thy father and thy mother.

This can go both ways in marriage. If you are blessed that

your parents are living, be sure to honor them in all you do. Remember to leave and cleave to one another as husband and wife, but that does not mean ignoring your parents. Treat them lovingly. If the in-law situation is a little uncomfortable or there are multiple in-laws due to divorce, be sure to show respect at all times. Bite your tongue until it bleeds.

As parents, you must work at this together. Be the best parents you can possibly be. Make time with your children, especially electronic-free time away from the TV and Xbox. Listen to your children and allow them to share things about their day, week, or life. If it is an option with work schedules, have family dinner on a daily basis. Family dinner is time set aside for the family to mold and gel. Do not allow your children to monopolize your marriage, but recognize the importance of being great parents so that your children will want and choose to honor you when they are adults.

THE CHALLENGE

Take your marriage journal and write some reflections on the first five Commandments. What did you learn about yourself? What could you be doing differently? Then during your weekly meeting, talk through some of the insights you had that were in support or violation of these Marriage Commandments.

VERSE TO REMEMBER

"Now therefore, amend your ways and your doings, and obey the voice of the Lord your God" (Jeremiah 26:13, KJV).

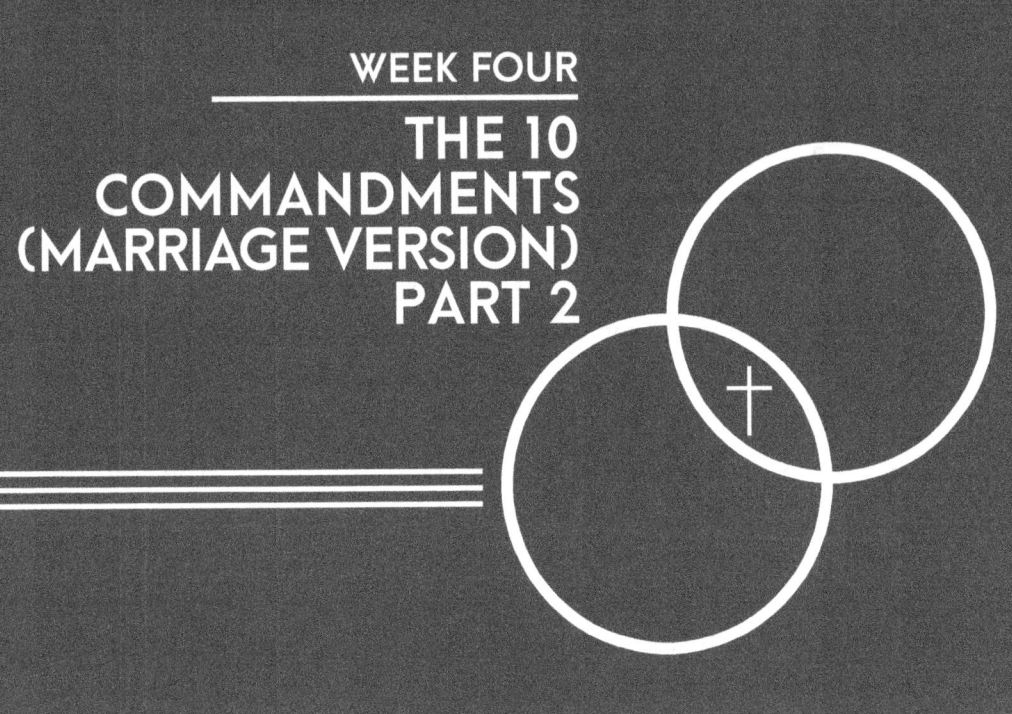

WEEK FOUR
THE 10 COMMANDMENTS (MARRIAGE VERSION) PART 2

How did you do last week as you worked through the first five Commandments? It's time to move on to the nexr five, so here goes.

6. Thou shalt not kill

This one is not so easy to discuss. Death in marriage is divorce. Divorce doesn't occur overnight. It is a final destination reached after a stressful, strife-filled journey. You add to the possibility of divorce every time you purposely pick at your spouse. I know no one out there purposely annoys his or her spouse, but I also know it is usually a compilation of little things, not one big incident, that kills a marriage.

Thou shalt not kill your marriage. Pride, ego, haughtiness, jealousy, envy, and strife will kill your marriage. Instead, apply abundant quantities of love, prayer, and peace. See your spouse as your partner rather than your enemy. Even if you view your spouse as your enemy, Jesus told you to love your enemies — so you are trapped in love either way. Remember that God intended the things he says and the things she does for your good, so you can grow and become more like Christ, who forgave and loved no matter what.

7. Thou shalt not commit adultery.

This is a given. Adultery waters down the love you have for one another. It depletes the exclusivity and makes the other spouse feel as if he or she is not your exclusive romantic focus. The Bible is clear on what you have to do when tempted: "Resist the devil, and he will flee from you" (James 4:7). If you sense any level of flirtation, even the smallest desire or lust, I have one word of advice: *Run*. I will go even further and implore you to avoid those you recognize have a "crush" on you. Although it may stroke your ego and make you feel good, it has a negative effect on your marriage and the enemy will use that temptation against you when you least expect it.

Dare I add pornography here? Porn, used with or without your spouse, diminishes the power of healthy marital intimacy. The perversion grows and creates an insatiable appetite that invades the wonderful bond between two individuals who exclusively commit to one another sexually. I'll be the first to say that anything goes in marriage (as long as you both consent) except for adding others. Pornography invites others into your private intimate space, creates an unnatural level of comparison, and a negative and false portrayal of sexual intimacy.

8. Thou shalt not steal.

You steal in marriage when you take something away from your spouse. This can be the drug addict who takes family money to acquire his drug of choice as well as the shop-a-holic when she does the same (and the problems I mention are not gender specific).

You also steal from your spouse when you make them feel bad about who he or she is. Allow me to clarify. Later in this book, we discuss the importance of understanding the concept behind the *Five Love Languages*. This book is a quick and easy read that helps identify both you and your spouse's wants and needs. Once you know your spouse's wants and needs and refuse to grant them, or even worse, purposely target to withhold from them, you are stealing from them. You are stealing from their self-esteem and self-worth, and trying to break their spirit. There is no love in the desire to harm one another.

9. Thou shalt not bear false witness.

Lying has no place in marriage. I heard it said once, "The only thing worse than being lied to, is realizing that the liar did not view you as worthy of the truth." Love your spouse enough to always tell the truth. Lies are always revealed. As the Bible says, "For everything that is hidden will eventually be brought into the open, and every secret will be brought to light" (Mark 4:22, NLT). It is more painful to have a secret exposed than to simply reveal it yourself.

10. Thou shalt not covet.

The grass is *never* greener on the other side. I heard a preacher say once, "The grass may look greener, but that's only because you can't see the poop from here." You must learn to be satisfied with what you have. Be satisfied with your spouse and everything about him or her. If this is difficult to keep in mind, then begin a gratitude journal where you can document the reasons you are thankful for your spouse. The positivity will help change your perspective in times of trouble. The Bible specifically mentions not coveting your neighbor's wife (or husband). Don't fall for the faulty thinking that the "other person" doesn't come with a lot of baggage. They do, and you will be adding to that baggage with an affair or a divorce and remarriage.

THE CHALLENGE

Just as you did with the first five Commandments, take your marriage journal and write some reflections on the last five Commandments. What did you learn about yourself? Then during your weekly meeting, talk through some of the insights you had that were in support or violation of these Marriage Commandments.

VERSE TO REMEMBER

"Let us search out and examine our ways, and turn back to the Lord" (Lamentations 3:40, NKJV).

WEEK FIVE
"I DIDN'T THINK IT WAS CHEATING."

I recently read the story of a man who received oral gratification from a random woman at a party. His response when asked why he didn't share it with his wife was, "I didn't think it was cheating." With ignorance or denial of this magnitude, let's create some parameters and guidelines of the irreducible components of what is called "cheating" on your spouse.

1. *Avoid any form of physical touch beyond a friendly cautious hug or handshake.* When private parts are exposed and fondled in any way, you are officially cheating.

2. *Avoid relationships you look forward to more than being with your spouse.* I'm not talking about the night out with the fellas or lady's day. I'm not even speaking of liaisons during which you plan to have a sneaky rendezvous of some sort (that, however, is cheating). I'm speaking of that daily meeting you find yourself looking forward to at work, or the response you get from ordering his special coffee each day because you were getting yours anyway. Intelligent adults can recognize the warning signs when you take the time to think about it.

3. *Avoid anything you wouldn't do in front of your spouse,*

which includes the flirtation, the compliments, and even some of the playful banter. I'm sure this wonderfully wise young man who "didn't think it was cheating" would never participate in his escapade in front of the wife who he claims to love so much.

4. *Avoid situations for which you begin to manufacture excuses.* When people notice and begin to call you names like "work spouse" or "second husband and wife," it is time to make some changes. If you find yourself doing things for that individual that you only do for your spouse, there is a problem.

Extramarital affairs are one of the top reasons for divorce among married couples. It is a violation of the marital bond and leaves painful reminders of failure in the relationship. Many people internalize extramarital affairs. Whether it is the perpetrator or the victim, there is often some level of blame placed on both by both. Sadly, extramarital affairs are truly the enemy's number one way to destroy the bond that should hold two people together for life. The Bible frequently addresses the power in two (see Ecclesiastes 4:9-12 and Matthew 18:19-20). When a marriage is torn apart, we sacrifice some of the spiritual power we have as a couple.

Extramarital affairs have been happening since the beginning of time, and the enemy continues to deploy this strategy because *it still works*. Everyone thinks it can't happen to them until it does. Affairs hurt all who are involved, and even those who are innocent bystanders; there is no winner and everyone loses. When you find yourself in the midst of even just getting close to the fire, *run!*

THE CHALLENGE

Be proactive about saving your marriage by following these steps to avoid "cheating".

1. Cut off all contact with the other individual.

2. Seek counseling for you individually and as a couple to figure out where the root of the problem originates.

3. Find an accountability partner.

4. Think through the future. Think about the pain this will cause your spouse, your children, the extended family, the church, and any relationship that has anything to do with you and your spouse. Sometimes people underestimate the pain an affair inflicts on others. Think about that before you go there.

5. Also consider the pain inflicted on your Savior and the bruising of your witness that will result.

6. Finally, think about Tyler Perry's 80/20 Rule from week one. Your spouse provides 80% of what you need and want. The affair provides about 20%. Who in their right mind would risk losing 80% simply to gain 20%?

Take the time this week to write about the "what ifs" where an affair is concerned. Use the list above to write about who would be hurt, who would change their opinion about you, and what both of you would lose. Also, take the time to write about the 80% your spouse gives you. What is the good about your spouse and your marriage? When the two of you come together, talk about what you have written.

VERSE TO REMEMBER

"Nevertheless let each one of you in particular so love his own wife as himself, and let the wife *see* that she respects her husband" (Ephesians 5:33, NKJV).

WEEK SIX
EACH ONE TEACH ONE

Although I don't know exactly where this saying originated, it has been considered an African proverb carried to America and included in African American community values. The whole premise advocates mentoring one another rather than depending on some system or organization to do it. It refers to the responsibility of the older generation to take on a mentee and teach them all they know, since hindsight provides 20/20 vision. What if we applied this saying to marriage?

What if every couple who was married more than ten years took on the responsibility of mentoring a couple who was married less than five? Then if each couple who's been married more than 20 years took on a couple who was married under 20 years and so on and so on? This would provide every couple some friendship, camaraderie, a listening ear, and a shoulder to cry on. It would help a struggling couple make it through and a stable couple laugh at themselves for petty disagreements. Couples would be able to be vulnerable and, most importantly, to grow.

The concept is more biblical than you may realize. Take a look at the lives of Elijah and Elisha, Eli and Samuel, and even Mordecai and Esther. These are examples where mentoring made a great difference in the lives and destinies of those individuals. Wouldn't it be great to make the difference in someone's marriage?

The idea is for you to take time to be with a couple who has less experience than you in this great adventure called marriage. The other side of this challenge, however, is to avail yourself of the mentorship provided by a healthy couple with more experience than you. This means a willingness to watch, listen, and learn the little things that make marriages work — things like the way he rubs her feet at night or she gets up and makes his coffee before he leaves the bed. These are the all-important acts that make or break a marriage. This is also a willingness to be told when your "stuff stinks." You give that couple permission to confront you about your mess without offense or retaliation. The most important point in these relationships is actually building "relationship." This will hopefully develop into a long friendship between couples that make their marriages easier to navigate.

THE CHALLENGE

Your mission for the week (and the rest of your life) is to identify two couples and get down to the all-important work we will term "Each one teach one." You will need one couple who has been married for a shorter time than you and another who has been married longer. The younger couple will be your mentees and the older are your mentors. Recognize that this does not involve the work of actually teaching, but rather it involves the work of organically building a relationship so you can watch and learn how to have an effective marriage. I realize the beginning of these relationships can feel unnatural, but press beyond that to make the relationship as natural as possible. When you find these couples, get together for dinner and explain what you would like to do, and get them to sign on to work with you. Don't give up if the first couples you approach aren't interested.

VERSE TO REMEMBER

"As iron sharpens iron, so a man sharpens the countenance of his friend" (Psalm 27:17, KJV).

WEEK SEVEN
THIS TOO SHALL PASS

"This too shall pass" is a statement I often heard older folks share when anyone was going through a tough time. When my boss was being so difficult that we all wanted to quit, a colleague said to me, "This too shall pass," pointing out that principals get shifted around, but we, the teachers, serve as the consistent foundation. When a curriculum was introduced that made no sense, someone said, "This too shall pass." Educators love to buy into the hot new trend, but somehow always fall back on the old faithfuls of phonics, grammar, and a basic foundation of fact fluency.

Now let's apply this maxim to marriage. God intended you and your spouse to live a life together 'til death do you part. He didn't say it would always be easy, but it has great rewards (obeying God always does). When the road gets rocky, you need to remember that saying and remind yourself that eventually whatever you are going through will pass.

When arguments seem to take over every conversation with your spouse: *this too shall pass!*

When the money's not right and it looks like you won't make it: *this too shall pass!*

When he's working all hours and you haven't seen one another in weeks: *this too shall pass!*

When she's more interested in the children than in you: *this too shall pass!*

When issues with the kids have you both at odds as to the solution: *this too shall pass!*

And when divorce seems imminent and it looks like you're past the point of no return, scream: *this too shall pass!*

Marriage is not a straight path. It's a roller coaster filled with ups and downs, twists and turns. Plan to ride the roller coaster together and laugh when it's moving so fast that you find your stomach in your throat. Trust God when the tunnel is so dark that you can't see the light of day. Believe that you both are more than conquerors in your marriage (see Romans 8:31-39), and let nothing separate you.

THE CHALLENGE

Spend this week researching Scripture verses that will help you when the going gets tough. You may choose to do this together or separately, but remember to come together with the verses you discovered to encourage, motivate, and inspire one another to stay the course when the going gets tough. You may choose to post these somewhere in your home so that you can easily get to them. I have a friend who actually turned her favorite verses into works of art by framing them, then placing them on display. This may not be for you, but if it is, make it a project you can do together, then find the place to display these. There is also a list of encouraging verses from the Bible included in Appendix One on page 153 to get you started.

VERSE TO REMEMBER

"Blessed is the man who endures temptation; for when he has been approved, he will receive the crown of life which the Lord has promised to those who love Him"
(James 1:12, NKJV).

WEEK EIGHT
MONEY, MONEY, MONEY, MONEY, MONEY

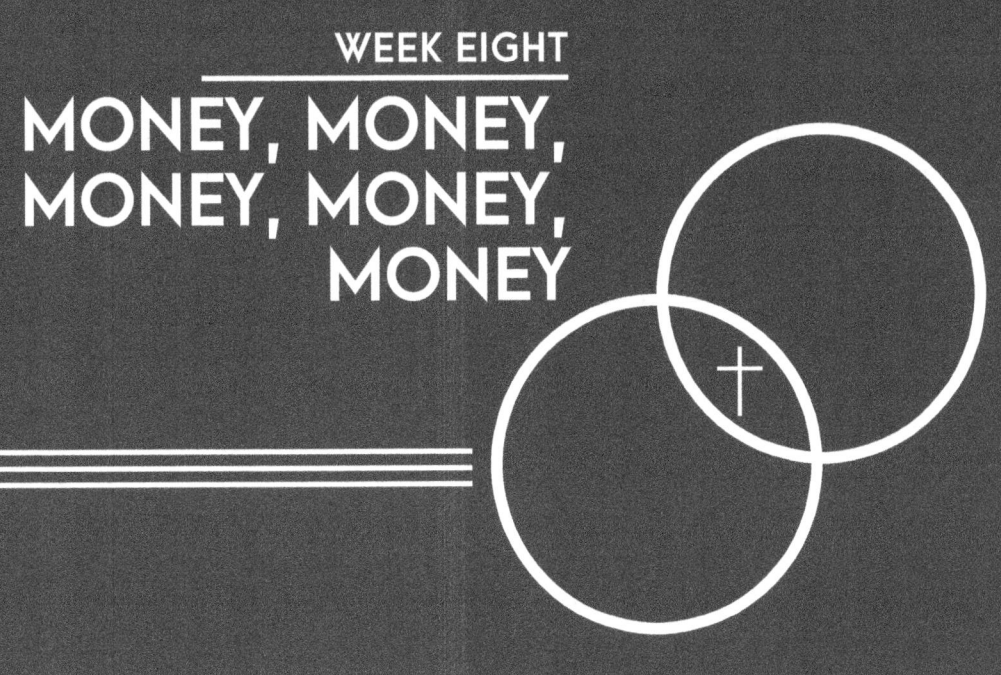

Did that title make you sing the song made famous by The O'Jays? That was the intention. It is a song fitting for marriage.

Some marriages will end in divorce due to financial strain and pressures. This occurs among couples who are rich, poor, and everyone in between. Mismanagement of money and miscommunication over finances can lead to the tragic downfall of a wonderful relationship.

Money reveals our personal life values. Those values are formed over a lifetime as we experience life and view how money affects our relationships, purpose, and self-esteem. For example, a child who grew up poor and lived in a housing project may become a frivolous spender. He may feel he has made it since he has a house and a job, so he wants the things he's never had, or more importantly for him, he wants to provide these luxuries to his children — despite the fact this may mean living far beyond his means. Or the complete opposite may be true: the girl who grew up in poverty may hold on to money tightly for fear she may not have enough if she doesn't. These are two extremes, and of course there are a host of other factors that develop our relationship with and understanding of money.

We are also influenced by how our parents spent or saved.

MARRIAGE CHALLENGES

Have you heard the saying, "More is caught than taught"? In other words, children do what their parents do more often than what their parents tell them to do. Parents don't always realize the habits and attitudes they are passing on to their children.

When your money issues are merged with the money issues of your spouse, fireworks are often created. If one spouse believes in having an emergency fund equal to six months of salary and the other lives by the motto, "If we have it, let's spend it," you are headed for some interesting financial discussions.

Money issues are often the trigger behind arguments over other things. You may be arguing while fixing the faucet because if he had listened to you and saved enough for a plumber, you could easily get it fixed. Or you're barking at each other about the car repair that can't be made because when he said, "Don't buy the pair of Italian leather boots because you need a rainy day fund," you did anyway, not realizing the rainy day was only a few hours away.

This is where a serious heart-to-heart talk has to take place. Will you merge all of your monies into one account? Will you keep separate accounts or will you each have a separate account and one joint account? Who is responsible for which bills? Is there one bread-winner or will both spouses work? If so, how much money will go where and on what date? How much will be saved? I know these questions seem boring, but the more detailed your plan, the less likely it is that money will come between the two of you.

I recommend seeing some type of planner or researching some plans online. Suze Orman has great online resources for couples to use. I don't earn any money for endorsing her resources. I simply appreciate what works and like to share it with others. She has questionnaires and surveys, as well as step-by-step guides available, to plan your best financial married life. I would love to go into what works for us, but what works for me might not for you. We do have a plan, however, and we have had to answer the questions I raised above.

THE CHALLENGE

This may be a little difficult, but this week sit down with all of your finances and share, discuss, and then come up with a financial plan for your marriage. This may include a budget, or a decision to make separate financial decisions. I am not a financial planner so I will not act as if I can grant financial advice, but I can say there has to be some conversation in your household about what is taking place financially. If an argument ensues every time you attempt to go there, you may want to utilize a financial planner of some sort.

I have included some of the questions and forms from an estate planner for your perusal and use in the Appendix. I have the interactive version available on my website. If you feel up to it (and it won't end in a knock-down, drag-out fight), I urge you to use those forms in the coming week to develop a plan for your household.

VERSE TO REMEMBER

"Owe no one anything except to love one another, for he who loves another has fulfilled the law"
(Romans 13:8, NKJV).

WEEK NINE
OUR MONEY PLAN

Maybe I *will* go ahead and share a bit about how Sheldon and I manage our finances. We have four primary bank accounts. I have one of my own at my job's credit union, he has one at his credit union, we share one at a separate credit union, and then we have a joint business account for our real estate company. We don't follow the norm that states we should disclose everything to one another. We don't tell each other much about our separate credit cards or purchases. We have a certain amount of money that goes into our joint account. Then we can spend the rest any way we see fit. I should also add that we learned a lot along the way, and this hasn't always been the perfect plan for us.

The downfalls to this plan are:

- My husband has always been responsible for all of the extra expenses. We didn't negotiate who pays the bills when they are higher than our original plan, which left him always paying the extra.

- If one of us is injured or incapable of paying bills, we're not totally aware of what needs paid and how it gets done.

- Lack of full disclosure (accountability) can lead to dishonesty or inappropriate spending.

My husband's control and his spend-first-tell-me-about-it-later norm, and my lack of discipline in spending and saving, are what makes this the best plan for us. We have also gone through a major life change. Our baby girl moved out, so we are transitioning from raising children to having an empty nest, and this has changed how we spend and save. My initial thought was we would have more money available to us now, but I quickly realized it's actually the exact opposite. Even grown kids can be budget busters.

THE CHALLENGE

This week, continue the work of digging into your finances. Develop the dreaded B word, a "budget." Turn to Appendix Three on page 165 or go to my website, www.leavingalegacyoflove.com, and pull up the budget paperwork. If you are a two-income household, you will need three copies of these forms, one for each of you and one joint form. Use the individual sheets to document your information and what a budget would look like for you personally, then bring those together in order to create a joint budget form. This exercise may not be necessary for you because you have already done this and feel comfortable with your finances. If this is the case, use this as a special date week. This could be a "get dressed up and go out" date, or a put on PJ's and sit on the bedroom floor snacking together. If this is an area you need to work on, however, use this time to your advantage, even if that means calling in a financial planner or impartial third party.

VERSE TO REMEMBER

"The plans of the diligent lead to profit as surely as haste leads to poverty" (Proverbs 21:5, NIV).

WEEK TEN
THE MARRIAGE I WANT, NOT THE MARRIAGE I HAVE

    I was talking to a woman recently who was quite complimentary toward my marriage. It was good to hear, but I was thinking, "If only she knew." She told me how my husband and I look like the perfect couple. She said we must be so happy together and then said that we must wear the most amazing matching sleepwear (I know it was a little too much for me too, but I just smiled and didn't respond).

    She talked about my blog and how she sees us doing everything it says when reading it. That's when I interrupted to explain, "Sorry to disrupt this fairy tale (especially since I was loving the fantasy, too), but I write about the marriage I *want*, not the one I *have*."

    Yes, I fantasize about the marriage where the house is spotless and all the cars have a full tank of gas all the time. I want the marriage where everyone wakes up bright-eyed and upbeat, longing to see one another. I want the marriage in which every hour or so I get a text that says, "I love you" or "I miss you" or "Girl, you're wearing that dress" (I wouldn't want my husband to say it like that, but I trust you get the point). I crave the marriage where he instantly and honestly answers "no" when I ask, "Does this dress make me look fat?"

    We are by no means the perfect couple. We struggle to put into practice the strategies we've learned and freely share with others.

It is always easier to tell people the right way to do something than it is to do it yourself. We argue, fuss, and fight; I am as sarcastic as the day is long (you can take the girl out of the hood…). We get consumed in other things and find ourselves forgetting to put our marriage first; and sometimes we are just plain mean to one another.

The key to our lasting marriage is a lot of love and a lot more God. We don't leave it to chance, because we know our flesh will fail every time, but God never will, so we pray a lot. I share all of this so you also will turn your marriage over to God, like we have done. In our hands, marriage is fragile and easily broken, but in His hands, it will be protected from the fiery darts of the enemy. I also share this to say that it's okay if you mess up. When you do, pick yourself up and dust yourself off, but never, ever give up on your marriage.

THE CHALLENGE

This week, take time to get to know what your spouse really wants from you. Learn how you can be the partner he or she wants and desires. Discover what you can do and say differently, as well as what you can avoid saying and doing. Sometimes we think we are serving our spouse when in actuality, we are simply giving him or her what we want instead of what they want. Use this time to take it all in. I know you feel as if you have done this before, but since you have a lifetime together, how about accepting this exercise again with the view that each of you has had time to come up with a more thorough list? Talk about it, pray about it, and then do your best to produce what your spouse says he or she wants you to. Don't do this under duress or grudgingly, but with the sincere desire to be the best spouse you can possibly be, not according to your definition but to that of your partner.

VERSE TO REMEMBER

"He who dwells in the secret place of the Most High, shall abide under the shadow of the Almighty"
(Psalm 91:1, NKJV).

WEEK ELEVEN
20 QUESTIONS MARRIAGE VERSION

Twenty Questions is a game people have enjoyed for years. The rules are simple: one person chooses an object and the others have to figure out what it is by asking a maximum of 20 questions. For the marriage version, the object is to get to know as much about your spouse as possible (and he or she about you).

Why this variation of 20 Questions? I advise you and others like you to get to know your spouse through date nights. This version of 20 Questions is an actual plan you can use on one of those date nights that will help the two of you delve deeper into your knowledge of one another.

Here are the rules for the game:

1. **Ask all questions with no malicious intent.** You want to get to know one another, not offend or vent to one another.
2. **Make a real date night of it.** Get dressed up and made up. Going out may not be the best idea as some questions go a little deeper than others and require a more private setting. Decorating a space in your house and deeming it off limits for everyone else may make it a great experience.
3. **Listen to your spouse's answers instead of searching for a re-

sponse or a reason why his or her answer is wrong.** There can be no wrong answers. The responses are your spouse's perspective, not what you think your spouse's perspective should be.
4. **Answer each question honestly.**
5. **Have fun.** Take this time and learn from it, but most importantly, enjoy getting to know one another and strengthening your marriage.

Here are some sample questions, but please don't limit your questions to this list.

1. What is your favorite color, food, dessert, car, number, movie, TV show, etc...?
2. What was your most embarrassing/funny moment?
3. Why did you marry me?
4. What do I do that makes you happy?
5. What do I do that makes you sad?
6. What do I do that makes you angry?
7. What is so special about me?
8. How do you describe me to other people?
9. How do you feel I support you?
10. What do you feel I could do to support you more?
11. What is one thing you wish you could say to me?
12. Is there something about your past or present you wish I knew?
13. What are your dreams for the future?
14. How can I help you accomplish that dream?
15. What do you like to do together (other than the obvious)?
16. What are ten things on your bucket list?
17. What is your dream vacation?
18. Open question (ask that question you've always wanted to know but never had the nerve/opportunity to ask).
19. Where do you see us in five, ten, twenty years?
20. Let's make a plan to make our marriage last forever.

You caught me. Number 20 isn't a question, but it is a great idea to make a plan for the future. This could be a list of things you're going to do, or stop doing. This could also be a plan for how you both would like to see your relationship develop and grow.

THE CHALLENGE

Use this simple game to create your best date night ever. As you answer each of the questions, take special note of the questions for which you had similar answers. If these items include something you can do (a trip, an activity, an adventure), you may want to take the time to begin planning how and when you can actually make it happen.

VERSE TO REMEMBER

"Fulfill my joy by being like-minded, having the same love, being of one accord, of one mind"
(Philippians 2:2, NKJV).

WEEK TWELVE
LIFE'S TOO SHORT

The older we get, the more we should realize life is too short to focus on petty disagreements or arguments. Life is too short to pass up opportunities to grow and to learn. Life is too short to spend another moment holding a grudge or seeking revenge.

Most importantly, life is too short to live in misery. Am I saying it's time to get a divorce because your spouse makes you miserable? Heavens no! What I am saying is that it's time to change your perspective and figure out how to make your marriage work. It's time for your marriage to thrive rather than just survive.

"How does that happen?" you ask. Well, let's look at a few ways:

1. Talk about it. You have been together for a month, a year, a decade, or more. You have to get to a place where you can actually talk about it to one another. Let your spouse know what you long for and what you need. Then listen as your spouse does the same. You will be surprised how much easier it is to understand your spouse when you actually listen to him or her. Use the information shared to improve your marriage and to fulfill the wants and needs of your spouse.

2. Just do it. Take everything you talk about and actually do it whenever possible. If your spouse says he or she needs you to give him or her a word of encouragement every day, just do it. If your partner says he or she needs a swift kick in the butt, just do it (that could be fun). And if they say they need you to be quiet and just be a supportive shoulder to cry on, just do it. Be willing to be everything your spouse needs and trust that they will in turn do the same for you.

3. Do something amazing together. Go on a mission trip and serve others, work together on a local service project, prepare food bags for the local food bank, or better yet, create your own way to serve the community. Serving others bonds you in a way that nothing else can. It causes a humility and a gratefulness to overtake you, and when that occurs with your spouse, you can't help but be thankful for that wonderful blessing God has given you in your marriage partner.

4. Do something crazy together. We recently heard the story of some senior citizens (married, of course) getting frisky in their neighbor's swimming pool. This is a great example of doing something crazy that bonds you and gives you a story that can be passed down from generation after generation. It also gives you a good laugh, and we all know, "Laughter doeth good like medicine" (Proverbs 17:22). I've said it before, but I'll include it here again: I don't want you to get arrested, but come so close that a police chase just might be involved.

5. Dream together. I heard Joel Osteen say, "Get around someone who makes your baby leap, not who puts your baby to sleep." Hopefully, that person is your spouse. Motivate, energize, and encourage one another to reach your dreams. Be the loudest cheerleader your spouse has and push him or her to the greatness to which he or she has been called.

While doing all of this, be sure to put God first and trust Him to strengthen your relationship even more. In God's hands, you can have an amazing relationship beyond what you ever thought possible. With Him, you learn to forgive and live. You learn to trust and believe, and you learn to love without limits. Recognize that life's too short so that you will make every moment count.

THE CHALLENGE

This week's challenge is to do something amazing and crazy together. It may take some time to plan it, but come up with something that will leave a memory that only you share. That could be a long hike, skinny dipping, a bowling tournament (complete with trophy and a cash prize), scavenger hunt, or movie marathon (watch as many James Bond movies as possible).

VERSE TO REMEMBER

"Why, you do not even know what will happen tomorrow. What is your life? You are a mist that appears for a little while and then vanishes" (James 4:14, NIV).

WEEK THIRTEEN
LET'S TALK ABOUT SEX

Salt-N-Pepa wrote a popular song that speaks about a topic once only hidden and discrete. While sex outside the confines of marriage is dangerous (and sinful according to God's word), marital sex should be a wonderful experience of two becoming one. There are no holds barred and everything is permissible. My pastor's term for this is the "fire in the fireplace" because it's cozy, comfortable, and warm, or at least it should be.

The problem comes in when we begin to see sex as a chore or an obligation. I never thought sex was an issue until I heard a friend at work complaining about her husband's birthday. She said, "Oh no, his birthday is coming, you know what that means!" I was in the dark because I did not know what she meant. When I asked, she went on to inform me that she was upset because she would have to have sex with him. I didn't react, but inside I was screaming, "Do you mean you only have sex *once a year*?" Who does that?

That was my wake up call to the fact that not every married couple has a satisfying sexual relationship. I noticed how Oprah and other talk shows would have a room full of women complaining about never reaching a point of climax, even after years of marriage. Other stories emerged of women who were either bored with sex or just had it rarely, sort of like a duty that they would check off their to-do list.

Surveys that indicate his or her marriage needs show the top need for men is sex while the top need for women is affection. The ideal situation would be for men to give affection as a prelude to sex, and for women to give sex in order to get affection, but it obviously doesn't work this way.

To improve this situation, let's actually take the time to talk about sex. Share the experience from your perspective after you have sex. What makes it enjoyable and what makes it not so enjoyable? What would you like to try? What do you want to stop trying? This is the time to be extremely (not brutally) open and honest. This is often uncomfortable (especially for Christians) because it feels raunchy or inappropriate, but you are talking to the love of your life. This is the only individual you will ever experience physically (God willing), so why not make that sexual experience as enjoyable as possible?

THE CHALLENGE

This week's challenge is to take the time to talk about your sex life. Since this is often an uncomfortable conversation, you may want to pull out the journal over the course of the week and write down everything you want to be sure to share. Be open and discuss with one another all of your likes and dislikes. Be adventurous and willing to try something new. Remember, however, not to go so far outside of your comfort zone that one of you is no longer able to enjoy the other. Then the most important part of this challenge is to put your plan into action as often as possible.

VERSE TO REMEMBER

"Let the husband render to his wife the affection due her, and likewise also the wife to her husband. The wife does not have authority over her own body, but the husband does. And likewise the husband does not have authority over his own body, but the wife does"
(1 Corinthians 7:3-4, NKJV).

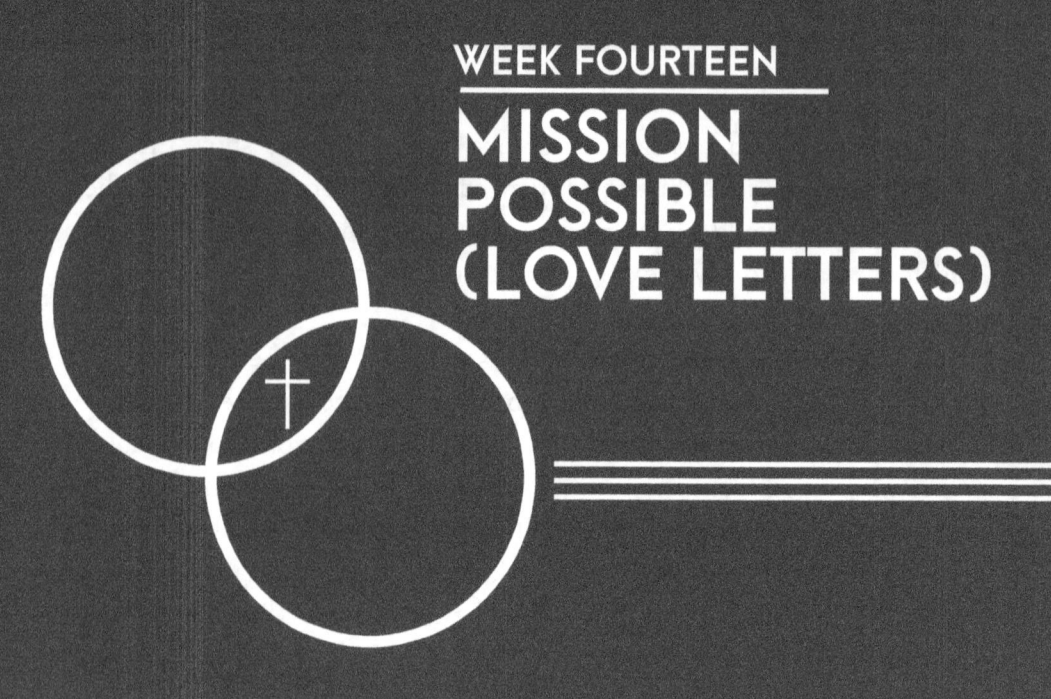

WEEK FOURTEEN
MISSION POSSIBLE (LOVE LETTERS)

Married couples can spend a lot of time arguing, fussing, fighting, and tearing one another down. This is counterproductive, because they then have to live in the environment they create. It is preferable that you spend time building your marriage rather than destroying it.

Writing love letters is a lost art because writing in general is a lost art. In just one generation, we've gone from writing by hand to inventive spellings and abbreviations in text messages, and then we use un-words that cannot be found in dictionaries.

Your focus this week is to write a love letter with pen and paper. The love letter is a tangible extension of you — your thoughts and emotions. It contains warm and fuzzy words, and is full of positive energy. Love letters can live on after you are gone, leaving a legacy of love for your children to read. More importantly, love letters are great for picking your spouse up when he or she is down. It reminds your partner that in this impersonal, cruel world, you think he or she is special.

Your letter should contain the reasons why you love your partner and share all the positives about your relationship. A good way to start before you write is with a list. This list should not be work, but simply some phrases and ideas you want to include in the letter, so don't worry about sentence structure or grammar at that point; just jot down what comes to mind.

List everything you love about your spouse - the way she smiles, the way he clenches his jaw when he's determined, the way she touches your arm when you're walking together, the way she wears her hair, and so on. Then make a list of all the things that make your spouse special. Follow with a list of why you love him or her, and close with a list of how he or she makes you feel special, loved, or admired.

Now that you have created your list, expand on those thoughts with descriptive sentences, and voila! You have a love letter. Be sure to proofread it to ensure that you are expressing exactly what you're feeling. Most importantly, enjoy yourself while writing words of endearment to the love of your life. This is your opportunity to make your spouse smile, so take full advantage of it by going all out.

THE CHALLENGE

Your mission is to write your spouse a love letter containing nothing but positive, lovey-dovey, mushy wonderfulosity!

VERSE TO REMEMBER

"Pleasant words are as a honeycomb, sweet to the soul, and health to the bones" (Proverbs 16:24, NKJV)

WEEK FIFTEEN
GOD FIRST

Marriage is a difficult balance of positive and negative energy. One day you're madly in love, and the next you can't wait to be left alone. Don't feel ashamed or confused because feeling this way is a common occurrence. It is difficult for two people to come together and become one, no matter how much in love they are. That is God's intention for marriage, however, and it's definitely possible, but extremely difficult. The good news is you have a lifetime to work it all out.

The only way this can be done effectively is for you to put God first. This helps you move away from pettiness. It reminds you that your relationship is a gift from God, not just a whimsical feeling based on your emotions. When you put the Lord first, you acknowledge that marriage is a ministry and not something that two people in love do with or to each other.

How do you put God first? There are many ways, but here are a few suggestions. Read them over and find a few that work best for you.

1. Pray together. Establish a routine time when you say a prayer together. Pray for your marriage, your family, for your life, and your love for each other. Pray for your church and the relationships around you, because healthy relationships have a positive affect on yours and vice versa. This doesn't have to be a two-hour intense prayer session. The most important thing is that you do it together and with sincerity.

2. Read the Word together. This could be a Bible verse to start the day or a more involved Bible study, whichever works for you. The important thing is that you study God's Word together. My church has taken on a challenge called *91 Weeks with Jesus* and strongly encouraged married couples to complete the program together. This Bible study includes a section of Scripture to read, which is then accompanied by a commentary from Dr. John Soper. This challenge is located online at www.mission119.org.

3. Attend church together. Be seen in church services as a couple. This serves notice to the enemy that as a couple, you live for God. When you listen to your pastor deliver God's word, you are both on the same page in spiritual matters. Talk about the service and the message that was given so you can learn from one another and grow together spiritually.

4. Talk about what you are reading in the Bible. Let your spouse know where God is taking you in your independent Bible study. Share what's interesting, confusing, and what stands out to you.

5. Share God-incidents. Since there are no coincidences in your walk with the Lord, share the God-incidents you experience over the course of your day. That would include things like the opportunities you had to share the gospel, the situations that allow you to be a blessing to others, or how others were a blessing to you. Take the time to share with one another all those God-ordained moments.

6. Pray for your spouse daily. Bombard heaven on behalf of that individual you vowed to love until death. When God blesses your spouse, you and your children will be blessed as well.

THE CHALLENGE

Apply as many of those suggestions as possible of how to put

God first, and then watch how quickly your love will grow for Him and for one another.

> ## VERSE TO REMEMBER
>
> "Seek first the kingdom of God, and his righteousness; and all these things shall be added unto you" (Matthew 6:33, NKJV).

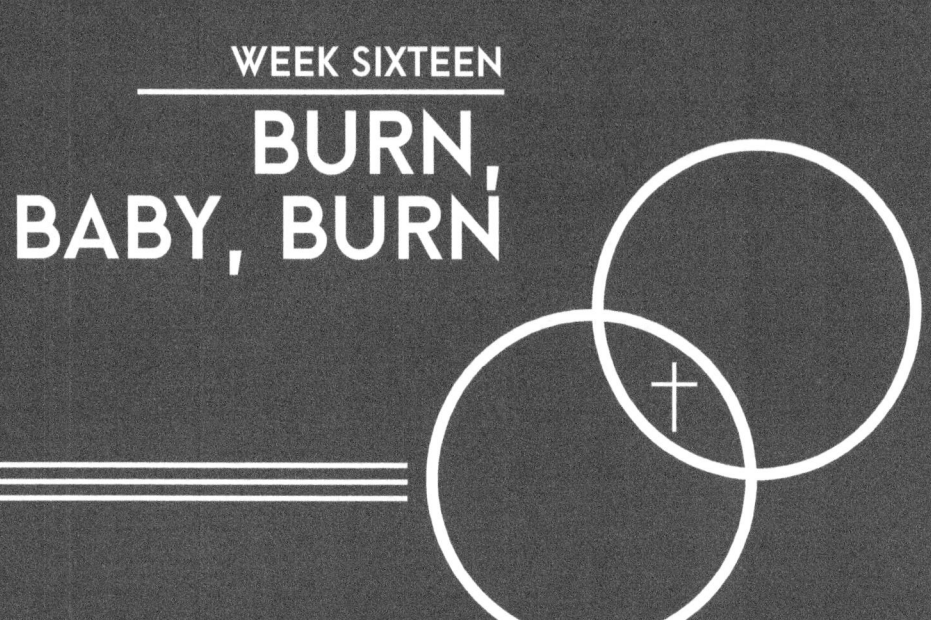

WEEK SIXTEEN
BURN, BABY, BURN

When you blow on a reluctant campfire, the added oxygen usually does the trick to get the fire going. This is where the term "fan the flames" comes from. When someone feeds a smoldering argument, we can also refer to that as fanning the flames. I want to apply that phrase to marriage and ask you to fan your flames of love for your spouse into a raging conflagration!

I am a middle school teacher, and the end of the school year is always stressful. Teachers have a deadline to post the entire year's grades, to document the attendance for a transient student body, to turn in supplies assigned them over the course of the year, and pack up their room as if they are moving out for good. When you add that to the stress of family life, it can drive everyone over the edge.

Recently my end-of-the-school-year stress was exacerbated by my husband's stress that he encounters with his job and the extra pressure he adds to his workload by being on several boards, being in the military, and working with various political associations. All of this created a powder keg in our house that with the tiniest spark of "Good morning" said the wrong way was destined to blow. We weren't headed for divorce court, but we were at each other's throats with some very intense fellowship.

I share this to implore you to make time for your marriage. Unplug from the daily grind and fan the flames of your marital love to keep that spark going. We recently returned from a cruise to Bermuda where there was no phone service and no Internet. After the initial culture shock of a new normal of not touching our phones every few minutes, we found ourselves settling into a romantic getaway where all we wanted was to share our next adventure with one another.

We stayed up until obscene hours either dancing or simply laughing and talking, and we rekindled the relationship we didn't even realize we were losing. We also became that touchy-feely-PDA (Public Displays of Affection) couple that so annoys us, but we couldn't help ourselves. Being accompanied on the cruise by a couple who are still in love after 42 years of marriage didn't hurt either. That couple let us know that it's possible to love one spouse forever and taught us not to sweat the small stuff.

THE CHALLENGE

Fan the flames of your marriage love by planning time away with your spouse. This can include going on an exotic vacation, or a trip one-hour away to the middle of the woods where there's nothing but the two of you. Unplug from the digital world by turning off all electronics and focusing on one another. Make it your goal to go home more in love than when you left. Refrain from all arguments. Think before you speak and be cognizant of how the things you do and say negatively impact your spouse. The most important thing for this day, weekend, week, or month is to fan the flames of your marriage in order to intensify the love you have for one another.

VERSE TO REMEMBER

"You have ravished my heart, my sister my spouse; you have ravished my heart with one look of your eyes, with one link of your necklace" (Song of Solomon 4:9, NKJV).

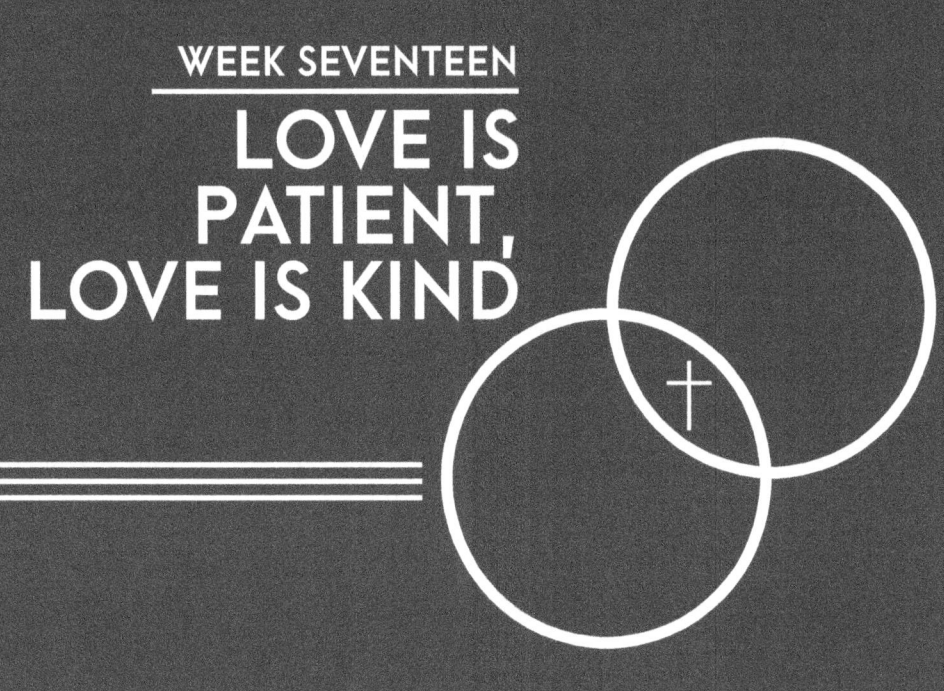

WEEK SEVENTEEN
LOVE IS PATIENT, LOVE IS KIND

Below are characteristics often identified as characteristics about love, which are much easier talked about than developed:

> Love is patient, love is kind. It does not envy, it does not boast, it is not proud. It does not dishonor others, it is not self-seeking, it is not easily angered, it keeps no record of wrongs. Love does not delight in evil but rejoices with the truth. It always protects, always trusts, always hopes, always perseveres (1 Corinthians 13:4-7).

Biblical love as defined in 1 Corinthians 13 is the cure for our affair-prone culture, so let's break down the passage above to learn how to avoid falling into the 20% category that makes affairs so attractive (see Week Two).

1. Be patient and kind. It is often easier to be patient with and kind to the people in your workplace who will forget your name two months after you die, than to be patient and kind with your spouse who will mourn your passing for years to come. You can put on a kind facade all day to enhance your career and chances for promotion, then go home and act out like you never would at work. The goal is to be kind and patient in both places, but especially with the one you vowed to love, honor, and respect.

Some affairs occur because someone is kind and shows attention to a lonely or hurting partner. Don't allow anyone to serve that role, and don't play that role for someone else. You be the kind face who is happy to see your partner every day. Fake it till you make it if you have to, but don't ever make your spouse feel like you could care less if he or she is present in your life.

2. Avoid pride at all costs. The Bible warns that "pride goeth before destruction, and an haughty spirit before a fall" (Proverbs 16:18, KJV). Apologize when you feel you are right for anything you may have done, and especially make sure to apologize when you are wrong. An apology is important because you want to heal the broken heart of the one you love. Don't allow your pride to destroy your wonderful relationship. When I look at couples in the puppy-love phase of their relationship, I notice how they regularly apologize to one another. They share the words that heal rather than words that hurt. There is no shame in their love. Since the Bible states that "he who finds a wife finds a good thing" (Proverbs 18:22), never allow pride to take your good thing away. This is also true for women. Pride can have you living in the same house and not speaking to that gorgeous man who you wish would just hold you all night. "Pride goes before a fall" in any and every situation, even marriage. Affair-proof your marriage by getting pride out of the way.

3. Never dishonor your spouse. Never bring others into your marriage issues and disagreements. In the heat of the moment, you can forget that you are having a temporary argument. When you share the negatives about your spouse with someone else, it often makes it difficult for them (the other person) to see the positive in your partner. When you and your spouse are back to being inseparable, those people will still see the no good dirty dog of a man, or the lying, scheming woman you told them about when your relationship was going through a low point. God designed your relationship to be private. If you aren't in a good place with your spouse, you don't have to lie and act as if everything is perfect, but never dishonor him or her by trying to get others to take sides against your partner.

4. Put the scorecard away. Don't hold the wrongs your spouse has done over his or her head. Forgive and yes, *forget*. This doesn't equate to pretending nothing happened. It simply means that you find a way to work through, talk through, and walk through issues together. Share the hurt the issue may have caused, but wipe the slate clean after the issue is worked out. If you've forgiven him for eating your last donut, don't flip out when he eats your last cookie and bring up the donut incident you said was forgiven (I know that's a simple example, but it gets at the point).

5. Be your spouse's ride or die. This saying simply means to be loyal no matter what goes down. Don't make your love conditional on how your spouse responds (or doesn't respond). Don't think, "I'll love you if you love me," or "I'll love you, if you're kind to me." Love unconditionally and love deeply. Love so deeply it hurts (in a good way).

Protect your spouse when they may be in harm's way. Trust your spouse at all costs. Hope and dream together with your spouse, and let your spouse know you are in his or her corner.

THE CHALLENGE

This week's challenge is to go through the list above and be honest about whether or not you are doing these well. Take the time to talk about the things you will do in order to improve your relationship by being more patient and kind.

VERSE TO REMEMBER

"With all lowliness and gentleness, with longsuffering, bearing with one another in love" (Ephesians 4:2, NKJV).

WEEK EIGHTEEN
JUST FOR THE HEALTH OF IT

I read an article that stated people who are married are healthier than singles, living an average of four years longer than singles. Some unhappily marrieds may be willing to lose those years to be single again, but I want those extra four years.

Many people believe this is a myth, but there are numerous studies that show companionship leads to improved health. There are also studies that indicate regular physical touch also contributes to a healthy life. These two factors — companionship and touch — would be enough to account for the longer life span, but the research behind the article presented a common-sense reason for the extra four years: Marrieds are more likely to "keep after each other to have regular checkups, take medicine, eat nutritiously, and so on" (Gottman & Silver, 1999). These researchers also identified some psychological benefits to being married, but that one stood out most to me. We actually nag one another into health. Someone please tell my husband that my nagging isn't all bad!

Why do I stress the health benefit of being married? I do so simply because it is one of the many benefits to being and staying married. God truly had a plan when He created Adam and then crafted (yes, I used the word *crafted*) Eve for Adam's health and wellbeing. Knowing this is the case, you should work to make your marriage as happy as possible, just for the health of it.

THE CHALLENGE

This week's assignment is going to seem a little out of place. The article I referenced pointed out that couples keep after one another to get their physical house in order. That is the goal for this week. If you haven't already done so, schedule the various appointments you may need to have. This means to call the doctor, the dentist, a counselor, a nutritionist, or whatever you may need to make this an amazing year. Join a gym together, employ a personal trainer together, or take a class on healthy eating, cooking, or exercise. Come together and talk about your scheduled appointments and plans for a new, healthier you.

VERSE TO REMEMBER

"Then the Lord God said, 'It is not good for the man to be alone. I will make a helper who is just right for him'" (Genesis 2:18, NLT).

WEEK NINETEEN
I SHOULD HAVE BOUGHT YOU FLOWERS

We live in a reactive society. Many of our rules and regulations come about because someone does something stupid, so then we make laws that will regulate the future so the stupid thing doesn't occur again. If we're not careful, we can find ourselves falling into the same pattern in marriage.

I was listening to Bruno Mars sing about his pain in the song, *When I Was Your Man*, as he reminisced about the little things his former girlfriend wanted from him. As I listened to him sing about buying flowers, holding her hand, and taking her dancing, I couldn't help but recognize that the things his girlfriend wanted weren't unreasonable. Since the song sold over eight million copies as a single, I also recognized his girlfriend is not alone in wanting those things from the man she loved.

How does it happen that we withhold what our partner requires? We know what our spouses want, but our pride, ego or selfish ways won't allow us to give that extra effort that will give them some joy. The sad reality is the issues of life can kill a marriage more slowly but more surely than any torrid love affair.

People enter marriage with one or two non-negotiable requirements, where they think, "If this happens, I'm outta here!" Those things could be an addiction, spousal abuse, or an extramarital affair. Those are major problems that will certainly destroy any relationship, but we often look past the seemingly less significant behaviors that can be just as destructive. What about neglect or rejection? What about constantly being made to feel bad about yourself? What about never seeing each other because you're so busy doing life? What about growing apart? My point here is that we need to work to avoid all things that will hamper or weaken our marital bond, not just certain major problems.

We never think marriage will become a monotonous routine, but it can become just that if we're both not proactive to keep things from ever getting that far gone. I know you're asking how you can be careful and proactive, so of course I have a list:

1. Recognize and apologize for your errors. Realize there is some degree of fault on both of your parts, so don't focus on who should take more blame. Instead, focus on yourself and what you've done, because you're the only one you can really change at the end of the day.

2. Make your spouse feel special every day. Pour it on thick. Life beats him or her up, and your job is to be there to pick up the pieces.

3. Show and tell. You can say you love me all day, but if you don't show me, save your hot air. Tell your spouse he or she is loved, and then back up your words with actions that prove your love commitment. If you're not sure about how to do this, ask your spouse how they'd like you to show love. It may turn into a good night of conversation and you might actually turn off the TV and spend time with one another.

4. Make time to be alone. Alone time means no cell phone, no TV, and no interruptions. Look into each other's eyes and get to know one another all over again. You have to define what this time looks like for you, but I can guarantee what you're not willing to do, someone else is.

5. Do something different. Get out of your comfort zone and do something your spouse enjoys. When my husband sits through a chick flick without an attitude, it makes me feel so loved. I'm sure when I go to his shoot-em-up, bang-bang movies without complaining, he feels the same.

This list could go on forever, but I'll close by imploring you to switch from a reactive attitude to a proactive one in your marriage. Make your marriage a happy place so you're not looking to a second marriage while moaning about what you should have done in your first one.

THE CHALLENGE

This is your week to pour it on thick and give your partner sincere compliments every day to make your spouse feel like the king/queen he/she is. You may want to create a list of everything that makes your spouse so wonderful. Use this list to give you some things to compliment in him or her. Then add to that complimenting by doing something to make your spouse know he or she is loved. Be creative without having to incur a major expense. Take time to think of what would make your spouse's day each day, and do it with no questions asked.

VERSE TO REMEMBER

"Love must be sincere. Hate what is evil;
cling to what is good" (Romans 12:9, NIV).

WEEK TWENTY
ACCOUNTABILITY

When should you find a marriage accountability partner? Should this happen when you find yourself in the midst of a difficult situation you can't seem to get yourself out of? Or should this occur before you even think you have a problem?

Many of the problems in marriage could be alleviated with an effective accountability partner. The enemy will always tempt you in the areas that work best: sex, money, and power. How you combat this is to not only turn to God, but then also to accept wise counsel from someone to whom you are accountable. My focus today is on sex, since that seems to be a major downfall for many. An accountability partner could be instrumental in helping you to watch out for these traps:

- A coworker of the opposite sex is having major problems in his or her relationship. They turn to you for a shoulder to cry on and a trusted ear. You find yourself in constant conversations about this individual's personal life and, although some of the conversations get uncomfortable, you continue the relationship in order to help. Sharing this with your accountability partner may give you a different perspective on the innocence of the situation or the blind spot you may have developed.

- A single friend needs help with something that requires you to go to his or her house to handle the situation. You told your spouse what you have to do and how long it would take, but find your time frame wasn't quite accurate. Rather than calling home, you try to hurry and get done so you can get home sooner. Or worse yet, you do not tell your spouse at all because you believe you already know he or she will have a negative reaction. Sharing this with an accountability partner may reveal the lack of trust that may arise from not giving your spouse the complete truth, or better yet, asking your spouse if they are okay with the situation in the first place.

- A coworker or friend of the opposite sex tells you that you are a good catch. He or she tells you how happy your spouse should be to have you, and if you had met a little earlier, you would be together. Having an accountability partner evaluate this situation might help open your eyes to the slippery slope this may be.

- A coworker or friend of the opposite sex tries to cheer you up by telling you how great you look or by sharing other accolades. Many times our ego doesn't allow us to see the difference between flirtation and sincere compliments. Honestly, sometimes what is said can fall into both categories. Knowing when to stop, drop, and roll (in the terms of the fire safety rules) is vital, and an accountability partner could help.

- You are tasked to take several road trips with a coworker of the opposite sex. Although everything stays platonic, you get to know one another very well and people begin to call you work spouses. A quality accountability partner could see this as a potential dangerous scenario.

- You are *the* man or woman at work! (Pronounced in the hood *da man*). Everyone laughs at your jokes, comes to you for advice, and seems to admire and respect you. In the midst of a heated exchange with your spouse, you find yourself saying, "Everyone else seems to like the way I am." Sharing this with an accountability partner may help you understand the fact that you may be drinking the proverbial Kool-Aid, and using it as a means to silence or manipulate your spouse.

These situations in and of themselves can be seen as innocent enough. Your enemy knows how to twist and turn the issues so things that aren't a big deal become a big deal. He also knows how to get you to the place where you let your guard down. A glass of wine with dinner turns into a bottle and the absence of a spouse leaves you susceptible to an inappropriate situation. How do you avoid this? You *run*! The word says resist the devil and he will flee from you (see James 4:7).

You know you're in a bad place when you have to question it, but you're in an even worse place when the questions stop and the defense begins. When we find ourselves defending this relationship rather than allowing the trusted friend to speak the truth that will expose the potential peril, we are in a sticky situation for sure.

The opening question was: "When should someone find an accountability partner?" My answer is, "Well before you know you need one." This partner is someone to keep you grounded, to help you through rough situations, and to tell you when something you are doing or thinking is just not right (or at least it appears that way). We are warned to "abstain from all appearance of evil" (1 Thessalonians 5:22), so don't be offended when someone questions how something looks that you are doing.

THE CHALLENGE

This week, your goal is to find an accountability partner of some sort. You may not think of someone right away, but the purpose is to intentionally get the search started. Pray about who this person may be and be proactive about finding him or her. If no one comes to mind immediately, some ideas for finding this individual may include joining a Bible study or small group in order to get to know a like-minded individual who is attempting to live life for Christ.

I implore men to find a male accountability partner and women to find a woman. I know that sounds old fashioned, but you want to avoid temptation and avoid the appearance that something funny is going on between you and a person of the opposite sex who is not your spouse. I also suggest this individual be married. I realize this is not always possible, but it is the best-case scenario simply because they share the marital perspective.

VERSES TO REMEMBER

"Therefore confess your sins to each other and pray for each other so that you may be healed. The prayer of a righteous person is powerful and effective"
(James 5:16, NIV).

"Brothers and sisters, if someone is caught in a sin, you who live by the Spirit should restore that person gently. But watch yourselves, or you also may be tempted. Carry each other's burdens, and in this way you will fulfill the law of Christ. If anyone thinks they are something when they are not, they deceive themselves"
(Galatians 6:1-3, NIV).

WEEK TWENTY-ONE
I WANT A DIVORCE

Are you tired of the toilet seat being left up, the toothpaste being squeezed from the middle, the hair left in the sink or worse yet, left in the shower? Have you had enough of the window being opened a crack when it's freezing outside or the "Oh honey, I forgot to take the garbage out," causing the house to smell for another week?

If any of this sounds familiar, then maybe it's time to consider getting some paperwork to say good riddance to that loser. Have you ever said or simply thought that divorce was the best option to get off this rocky road called marriage?

Did you forget about the fact, however, that he fills your tank with gas or she cooks your favorite meal every Thursday? Maybe your selective memory pushed out the fact that he mows the lawn with no coaxing, or she gets up before you leave for work, allowing you to sleep in as she gets herself and the entire family ready for the day? Do you also forget to recall the massages or foot rubs he gives when he knows you're stressed, or the attentive ear she gives when she listens to you vent about the same issue over and over again? These scenarios may not be exactly what you encounter, but you get the point.

In marriage, we take the good with the bad. We get the "for worse" along with the "for better" because marriage is not always easy, but it's always worth it.

The next time you're tempted to scream, "I want a divorce," have a talk with a single co-worker who is dying to have your life. Talk to someone who is either going through or fresh out of a divorce. Those talks may put some things back into perspective. The fact of the matter is the grass is only greener where you water it. Take some time to think about the good things rather than dwelling on the bad. You'll be surprised how gratitude and love can cover negativity and contempt when you allow them to do so.

THE CHALLENGE

This week you must accept the fact that you cannot change your spouse. This being true, ask yourself the question, "Since I cannot change my spouse, what can I do to make this marriage live-able?" This is not a "I may as well work on me because you are hopeless," but an acceptance that you may be contributing to whatever problem is between the two of you. Just be open. This needs to be a sincere "I am committed to work on my issues regardless of what you do" type relationship building. The proverbial "watering of your grass" is your purpose.

Before you sign on the dotted line to finalize a divorce, you will be asked, "Did you do everything within your power to make this relationship work?" Your task for the week is to do just that. Make it like honeymoon central. Love, talk, and be relational, with no expectations of reciprocal behavior on the part of your spouse.

This will be difficult, especially if you and your spouse have been at odds, but do it anyway. Do it as unto the Lord. You'll be surprised how God can use your obedience to change the heart of your spouse.

VERSE TO REMEMBER

"Above all, love each other deeply, because love covers over a multitude of sins" (1 Peter 4:8, NIV).

WEEK TWENTY-TWO
MAKE ME LAUGH

I'm giving away my age here, but there used to be a late night comedy show called *Make Me Laugh*. On this show, comedians were hired to make contestants laugh in a specific timeframe. The contestant who was able to hold out the longest won money and prizes. It was a pretty corny show, but I absolutely loved it.

Marriage is a roller coaster of ups and downs. It requires a complete change of lifestyle because you are never quite ready for what is to come, and you have to learn to approach everything with another person in mind. How much greater would our marriages be if instead of carrying negative energy and trepidation, we took on the motto of this show and set out to make our spouse laugh every day?

My husband and I have some pretty stupid inside jokes that make us fall out with laughter. For example, my grandson can't say his sister's name (Sydni), so anytime we say "Sinney," we laugh like teenagers. Anytime we add half to a number, we have to say "turtle" like we saw in a goofy movie we watched together. It sounds crazy, but it makes us laugh till we cry.

I share all of this to challenge you to find a way to break up uncomfortable, stressful, and even painful situations with laughter.

MARRIAGE CHALLENGES

Make it your goal to make your spouse spit his or her milk across the room as often as possible, since this adds to the personal bond of love you share together.

THE CHALLENGE

Start creating those inside jokes and stories to make your relationship more special than any other. A good game to play for this week is a version of the *Make Me Laugh* TV show. Get out a timer and for two-minute intervals, take turns trying to make your spouse laugh.

1. Set the timer for one minute.
2. Spouse one sits in a chair and attempts to keep a straight face.
3. Spouse two attempts to make spouse one laugh as hard as possible.
4. Time how long it took for a smile to crack.
5. Switch roles.
6. Feel free to include the kids in on the fun if they just won't go away.

Pictures or video clips may also be used to help create a happy memory.

VERSE TO REMEMBER

"A merry heart doeth good like a medicine:
but a broken spirit drieth the bones"
(Proverbs 17:22, KJV).

WEEK TWENTY-THREE
LOVE IN THE NEW YEAR

Every new year that you're still with your boo makes you an anomaly. While many have called it quits due to irreconcilable differences, you and your honey are holding on through thick and thin. It hasn't always been easy, but it will always be worth it. Life is too short to hold on to a grudge.

The theme for every year in marriage should be forgiveness. There are many issues in marriage and it's not always easy to forgive and forget, but if you don't, you are headed for trouble. Here are a few tips to help with the issue of forgiveness.

1. Keep in mind that each conversation with your spouse may be your last. We can avoid so many arguments if we lived every moment as if we'd never see one another again. We would approach conversations differently and do our best to cater to our spouse, or at least come to a quick resolution of touchy issues.

2. Talk, talk, and then talk some more. Spend time talking to each other about your ups and downs. Talk about what you like and what you dislike. Be your spouse's ear and shoulder to cry on, or someone else will. That's not a threat, just a precaution. Get to know everything about your mate and let them know everything about you.

MARRIAGE CHALLENGES

Develop a system to help you address issues by talking. Some people have a talking stick or microphone, some symbol that says the person with the mic or the stick is the only one who can talk at that time. This allows you to take turns and learn to listen to one another. An advanced step is for the listener to reiterate what he or she heard after the other person finishes. This creates a good environment for two-way conversation and discourages the temptation to interrupt or cross examine before the other person is finished.

3. Assume your spouse has your best interests at heart. I heard my friend, Joy Eaton, say this, and it caused me to pause and watch how the arguments and issues between my husband and me were playing out. Most of our issues come from a misunderstanding that begins when my husband tries to take care of me in some way. For example, not too long ago he finished the basement so we had more space for entertaining. In the midst of this remodeling job, the entire house was filled with drywall dust. Can you imagine his reaction when all I could do was complain about the drywall dust and not the wonderful project he took on? I'm sure you can think of situations when all your spouse wanted to do was something nice for you, but all you saw was the negative side of it. How many wives come home to a hot meal and complain because the kitchen is a mess? His intention was to do something for you, so learn to celebrate that.

4. Pray together. Pray for your marriage and with your spouse often. This can be uncomfortable and even the strongest of spiritual leaders sometimes have trouble doing this. Prayer is your greatest weapon against the enemy. The enemy of our souls knows that where two or three are gathered together in Jesus' name, God is in their midst. Make it your goal to pray together and for one another as often as possible. If you add Bible reading or a devotional to this time, the enemy doesn't stand a chance to come between you.

THE CHALLENGE

The task for this week is to develop a forgiveness plan. The first and most important part of this plan is prayer because God is the only one who can soften our hearts. For this week, your goal is to pray together for your marriage. Unlike weeks past, you are going to pray together each day this week. Make it your goal to pour out to God all of the issues you may have. Be careful not to attack the other person through prayer, but pray with the goal of building and strengthening your relationship.

VERSE TO REMEMBER

"And when you stand praying, if you hold anything against anyone, forgive them, so that your Father in heaven may forgive you your sins" (Mark 11:25, NIV).

WEEK TWENTY-FOUR
SEEN AND NOT HEARD

This was a saying that served as a norm for generations, and it indicated that children should not be involved in adult conversations. Of course, this seems harsh to the New Age parent who allows children to "express themselves" as they see fit. The reality of the previous norm is it spared children from having to deal with adult themes, and it allowed them to be children. That being said, this should be the ongoing rule for your marriage. I have counseled families who not only allow children to see them have knock-down, dragged-out arguments, but also even force the children to take a side in the dispute.

There are various ways in which this is done, so the key is avoiding all of them. Here are just a few (yes, another list).

1. Do not argue in front of the children. You know this is a bad habit, but in the heat of the moment, you can often forget, or simply choose to ignore it. This irrevocably damages children and builds insecurities within them they don't know how to cope with. Make a rule that intense arguments never occur in front of the children.

2. Do not ask your children what they recall about a particular situation in order to help prove your point. For example, don't ask you child something like, "Didn't your father say such and such?" If the child answers the question, he or she is taking your side and if they refuse to answer or conveniently can't remember, they are choosing your partner's side. Either way, the child loses.

3. Never allow your children to join in the argument. This is the ultimate no-no. It feels good to have a tag team, but consider what your child feels like. A child loves their parents equally and feels loved by both. The uncomfortable position of taking sides or the fear of disappointing a parent detracts from their relationship with Mom and Dad. Even worse, this can create an atmosphere in which the child feels comfortable, and is actually encouraged, to disrespect one of his or her parents. How then does that marginalized parent discipline or reprimand this child? It sets up an unhealthy atmosphere.

Remember, children learn what they live, so let your love for them help to make their childhood a happy rather than a harmful experience, and leave the adult situations to the adults.

THE CHALLENGE

Write in your journal about specific times when you involved your children in things that were beyond their years to handle or comprehend. We all have not-so-stellar parenting moments of which we are ashamed. Write about it. You may want to document what occurred, what caused you to react the way you did, and the outcome of your reaction. Repent about those situations. Sincerely cry out to God to teach you how to parent your children in a God-honoring way.

In your time together, develop a plan for consistently incorporating God-honoring activities into your parenting plan. This could include adding family devotions to your daily norm, doing a family Bible study (daily or weekly), or creating a family prayer time if it's not already established. You may have each person pray during each session or develop a schedule of who prays at each session.

VERSE TO REMEMBER

"Train up a child in the way he should go; and when he is old he will not depart from it" (Proverbs 22:6, KJV).

WEEK TWENTY-FIVE
SECRETS

    Many families have secrets that hold them hostage. These secrets explain things like why the adopted sister looks so much like the family (because she may be the product of an affair or a teenage pregnancy), and why brothers haven't spoken to one another in more than a decade (sometimes fighting over money, their mother's honor, or because one may not be Daddy's baby). Secrets bring pain, stress, and even hatred that serve to steal, kill and destroy, which are the ultimate objectives of the devil.

    Some secrets are worse than others. Molestation and incest are secrets common to many families, yet they remain hidden in the dark by all involved. Whether it's due to fear, embarrassment, or denial, families often carry those secrets to the grave.

    Why do I address family secrets in a book about marriage? When these secrets eat away at the victim, the repercussions carry over into every area of life. How do I know? Experience is the best teacher, and I have had moments when I wouldn't allow my husband to touch me because my mind was processing issues not related to him, issues that should have been dealt with long ago. I thank God that He helped me work through the pain rather than allowing me to run from it. "What we conceal God can't heal" is a true statement, not because He's incapable but because He's gentle and won't force Himself into any area we'd rather hide from Him (which is silly, because He already knows).

Perhaps it's time in your life to expose the enemy for who he is. Release those secrets that are causing you to die inside and causing a slow death to your relationships. Holding onto pain from the past won't allow you to be fully vulnerable to your mate, and that will cause shame, insecurity, and doubt to erode the foundation upon which you are attempting to build your life. Save your marriage by saving yourself.

THE CHALLENGE

Journal about some of the pains of your past. Dig deep here and allow these deep, dark secrets to be exposed by the power of the Light. Pray, read the Word and allow God to minister to these areas. Also, take the time and spend the money to find a good counselor or licensed listener to get those hidden pains out. This provides a safe space that is completely confidential until you are ready to share with a trusted friend or even other family members suffering through the same secret pain and shame. Reveal it so God can heal it.

When you come together, if this secret is something your spouse is not aware of, be willing to be vulnerable and share it. If this has been shared already, go deeper and share something about it your spouse may not know. When you are the listener, be compassionate and loving in order to be part of your spouse's healing.

VERSE TO REMEMBER

"They triumphed over him by the blood of the lamb and the word of their testimony" (Revelation 12:11, NIV).

WEEK TWENTY-SIX
THE FOO FIGHTERS

Please don't confuse this title with the famous rock band. In this situation, FOO represents the Family of Origin. When people get married, there is often the belief that this is the love of one's life. The giddy, puppy-love feeling is present and there's the theory that he or she can do no wrong. The thing we often forget to investigate is the family of origin (FOO) issues. I remember my grandmother asking one of my boyfriends about his upbringing. Being ignorant of that kind of wisdom, I was annoyed that she would go there. I was embarrassed for him and I wanted to "get out of Dodge" as quickly as possible. Now that I look back on that situation, I wish I would have applied her wisdom in all of my relationships.

This was important because she asked my boyfriend who his parents were, what they did for a living, what church they went to, what they believe, if they were still married, how many other children they have, and if they have children to other people. She went on to ask about his family line, which is where I stopped her and said we had to go. Silly me! What my grandmother knew that I did not is the family of origin is what makes you who you are. It is responsible for many of the good and bad choices you make.

I am not making excuses for anyone, but have you ever heard the saying, "more is caught than taught" or "children learn what they live." These sayings point to the fact that no matter how much your parents tell you something is wrong, if they do it, they are teaching you it's right. Your family of origin teaches you about relationships and how to live them, teaches you communication styles, teaches you how to love and who to love. Sadly, the family of origin also teaches who not to love, and it is where most people learn racism or sexism or any other -ism you can think of. If we took more time to get to know our potential mate's family history and family of origin, we could avoid many of the pitfalls we experience.

I say all this to emphasize that we need to explore family history and family of origin matters together. My internship supervisor taught me to make what's called a genogram. A genogram is a supersized family tree that not only lists who was in my family, but how the relationships between my family played out. I was able to trace lines of abuse, alcoholism, and drug addiction, as well as marital longevity and healthy relationship bonds. This information was revelatory for me because it helped me see how I developed some of the beliefs I have and how many of the patterns played out in my family (positive and not so positive). Seeing my husband's genogram also helped me see why he does some of the things he does and how his beliefs are also wrapped in his family-of-origin.

Take the time to get to know one another's family of origin. It will not only be interesting, but it will also be insightful. The fact of the matter is that if the two of you have or plan to have children, this will play an integral part in your children's future as well.

THE CHALLENGE

This week, I want you to research the concept of a genogram. There are a few websites that explain what they are and how to make them. There are even a few sites that will help you make one for a small fee, but the free ones are often just as effective. This week, take the time to create your genogram. Be sure to go at least one generation up and one generation down from you (two is preferred but not always possible). When you come together, make a night of sharing your genograms. Even if you have been with your spouse for a long time, you will learn something new about him or her and vice versa. Share openly and honestly everything you know about your family, and be receptive to hearing everything your spouse shares about his or her family.

Most importantly, use this time to discuss how these issues and experiences have shaped your lives. I titled this the FOO Fighters because many times there are things revealed that we may be embarrassed about or ashamed of. In order to break the curse and overcome many of the issues in our family of origin, we have to reveal that they exist and be willing to fight against them in our relationship.

Two websites that could possibly help you get started are www.genopro.com and www.genograms.org. Allow these to guide you through the process.

VERSE TO REMEMBER

"This is my commandment, that you love one another as I have loved you. Greater love has no one than this, than to lay down one's life for his friends"
(John 15:12-13, KJV).

WEEK TWENTY-SEVEN
LOVE HURTS

I hear people say love doesn't hurt, but I must disagree. Let me preface my taking exception by saying that if love includes black eyes and body slams, then I wholeheartedly agree — love shouldn't hurt in this way. Love should never include violence. When we are speaking of a normal loving relationship, however, it will often hurt like the dickens (I'm beginning to sound like my grandfather).

Love hurts because any time you fall in love, you succumb to a level of vulnerability with another individual. You let down your protective walls and give someone permission to either return the favor or to step all over your heart. In a mutually-loving relationship, we will hurt one another on a regular basis. This should never be your intent, but the truth is, two people with different likes, dislikes, hopes, and dreams will unintentionally offend one another simply because the one doesn't see life like the other does. Thus, they will do things innocently that the other will process as intentional or wrong.

My husband spent many years as a policeman. He adopted a saying, "Suck it up and drive on." When his teammates say that to each other, it makes them step out of their feelings and shake off offenses to continue their work. When he says this to me, I cry. He never sets out to make me cry, but when I have spent the day being reprimanded at work only to come home to three children who need me, and then hear, "Suck it up and drive on," it elicits nothing but tears. He had to adopt a more healing phrase.

Anything from choosing the wrong movie to not getting the "right" gift for Christmas can lead to pain and disappointment. The key is never to inflict intentional pain on one another. Never make it your goal to make your spouse cry or to hurt his or her feelings.

Finally, because love hurts, you must apologize often. Apologize when you're right and apologize when you're wrong. Apologize just for the sake of apologizing in order to be part of your spouse's healing. Love does hurt sometimes, so make it your goal to avoid that hurt at all costs, or to make it right when it happens.

THE CHALLENGE

This week's challenge is to spend the week documenting ways your spouse may have hurt you unknowingly, anything from laughing at the outfit you thought was cute to ignoring your story about how the boss gets on your nerves. Write each of the incidents down, but be sure to add what hurt about it. This is not a time to place blame, but rather a time to get into your spouse's frame of reference.

When you come together, share what hurt most, but most importantly why it hurt. Let me reiterate. This is not a time to place blame, but rather a time to get into your spouse's frame of reference. Listen to what caused the pain. You may even be able to find the root of the issue in order to keep it from happening again. For example, there may be a connection to a time when your family of origin laughed at an outfit you chose to wear, so when this happened again with your spouse, it triggered that memory. Since neither of you is a mind reader, neither one of you could have figured out why the other one got so offended, so the purpose of this week's challenge is to share. There is a saying, "You don't know what you don't know," but now that you know it, you can stop the behavior or offending practice. Refuse to reinjure your spouse by doing or saying the same thing again. Sincerely apologize and move on, having learned something new about the love of your life.

VERSE TO REMEMBER

"The words of the reckless pierce like swords, but the tongue of the wise brings healing" (Proverbs 12:18, NIV).

WEEK TWENTY-EIGHT
MARRIAGE CAN BE MESSY

While watching Tyler Perry's movie, *Why Did I Get Married*, I couldn't help but wonder how many people regularly ask this question. There are a myriad of reasons for couples to question their motives for getting married. After a while, petty arguments, issues with housekeeping, cooking, and tensions with in-laws and money (the big one) can cause anyone to wonder, "Why did I volunteer for this?"

I heard Lysa TerKeurst, president of Proverbs 31 Ministries, say, "Marriage can be messy" at the end of a radio broadcast and I thought, "She is so right!" The fights you didn't even know were fights until you found yourself breaking stuff and wondering later, "Why was I so upset?" You had a disagreement that was never meant to lead to a week without speaking, or calling him a name you didn't realize was still in your vocabulary.

My husband and I once had an argument that got progressively more intense. I should add that my husband is often the "wordier" one during our arguments, while I am the one who shuts down and simmers. Usually while I'm simmering, however, he is throwing shade (verbal jabs) in order to re-engage me. During this particular argument, I don't know what he said, but it struck a nerve, and I went straight from calm to rage in a matter of seconds. My saved, sanctified, Holy-Ghost-filled self, who hadn't used so much as a curse word in years, commenced to cussing with every word I could think of. I didn't even take a breath. I sunk to an inappropriate low that hurt my heart, his heart, but most importantly, the heart of God. It was embarrassing too, because I thought I was delivered from that type of conversation.

As the title of this chapter states, marriage can be messy. My mouth made a complete mess of everything we had built over the course of quite a few years. Remembering this now is a little comical, and we often share this story with couples both for comic relief and to let them know they are not alone if they too have had a blow up. We also share it to give those who haven't ever done something like this a warning of what *not* to do.

The key element that will help you deal with these messy marriage issues is love, forgiveness, and the Lord. These three together are the heavy-duty paper towels that can clean up your mess most effectively. It's difficult to remember you're in love when your spouse makes you angry, but it is vital to do so. Your goal shouldn't be to injure but rather to get to the root of the issue. Your spouse is not the enemy, he or she is the love of your life, and you want to treat them that way.

For those issues for which you can't seem to find a resolution, first and foremost, you must pray. Pray earnestly for your spouse, for the issue at hand, and for your relationship. Don't be surprised at how messy the two-becoming-one can be, and then finally, forgive, forgive, and forgive again.

THE CHALLENGE

This week, I want you to journal your thoughts about any areas of unforgiveness you may have toward your spouse (or others, for that matter). When you slip to a low like the one I wrote about above, there is probably some issue still brewing or some level of unforgiveness lurking in your heart. Write about the silly stuff and the serious stuff that bother you. Document anything for which you need to forgive your spouse. Once you have your list, strike a line through each one and write, "I forgive you."

When you come together to talk and when this list is something you are able share with your partner without an argument erupting, do so, but if not, just say to one another, "I forgive you," until you mean it. Close this week by having a time of earnest prayer, and then enjoying an evening with a heart free of any bitterness.

VERSE TO REMEMBER

"If we confess our sins, he is faithful and just to forgive us our sins and to cleanse us from all unrighteousness"
(1 John 1:9, KJV).

WEEK TWENTY-NINE
MAKE IT LAST FOREVER

As my husband and I approach our twenty-ninth year together and our twenty-second year of marriage, people regularly ask the same question: "How do you make it last?"

I am never really sure how to answer them. Let me rephrase that, I know there is not one simple answer to that question, so I don't know which answer to give them. My hubby and I have been through thick and thin. We've experienced a roller coaster of emotions as we have traveled on the track of life together. One day, we were young, starry-eyed, and madly in love, and then on another day we went out of our way to avoid having to speak to each other. Through all of this, however, we've stayed together. Since you know me by now as a list girl, I'll give you my answer to the question about how to make it last in a list format. Keep in mind that this list is not prioritized, it just contains my random thoughts.

1. Fall in love with the same person over and over again. Think about all of the great qualities your spouse has. Reminisce on the puppy-love phase of your relationship when you could not keep your hands off one another. Recognize the things that make him or her special, little things like the way he talks, the way she looks at you, that little hair that always falls into her eye when she's talking, the smell of his cologne, the way he touches the small of your back, and other such behaviors.

You love each other. This is the easy default answer to the question of how to make it last. Most couples start out in love. The problem is you don't really know what love is until that love is tested. Remember your vows that stated, "for better or worse" and "in sickness and health"? You won't know until you are awakened by a spouse who can't walk for some reason, asking for a bowl of ice cream in the middle of the night, or worse yet, cleaning up vomit from a sick wife who is exhausted because of surgery, chemotherapy, or pregnancy. You won't know what love is until you've gone through (and made your spouse go through with you) the traumatic weight-gain, weight-loss cycle. Hearing the agony of her reactions to the scale and enduring midnight workouts or hunger strikes can be draining. There are so many things that have tested our marriage, but they confirm the fact that we really do love each other. I wouldn't want to live without him, and I know he wouldn't want to live without me, even when living together makes us crazy.

2. Strive to make one another happy. I'm a girl who thinks spousal happiness is a top priority. I live by the sayings, "Happy wife, happy life" and "Happy hubby, life is lovely." We discussed this issue already, but if you want to make your marriage last, then work to keep one another happy. Don't demand that he make you happy before you will make him happy or vice versa. You should both be doing this simultaneously, actually trying to outdo one another.

3. Choose your battles. There was a time when our marriage could best be described as a battle of wills. We were willing to fight about any and everything, just to get our way. We eventually realized life is too short to be that miserable. We learned to choose only the battles we felt needed to be fought for sanity's sake and for the good of our relationship.

4. Be teammates. We have learned that it's us against the world. I've had friends stop talking to me for absolutely no reason.

I've even had friends start talking about me when I thought we were close. Through all of that, my husband has been the one constant in my life. He is, as the kids say, "my ride or die," and I have to treat him as such. Teams succeed when they work together, so that's what we had to begin doing. It's not always easy, but it's always worth it.

5. Date. We always find ways to get away by ourselves, just the two of us. Sometimes that involved driving to a park, sitting, and looking into each other's eyes. At other times, it involved shutting our bedroom door and reading a book. Whatever it took, we love being together. Our newest adventure (now that we are empty-nesters) is traveling the world side by side. We love it and use the time to build our relationship. You don't have to plan some exotic adventure to have an exciting date. It can consist of going out for dinner and a movie or just putting a blanket on the living room floor and eating your romantic microwave dinner there. Pour life into your marriage in these times so when the going gets tough, your marriage will have strong legs on which to stand.

6. Sex is key. One of my favorite verses is, "Marriage is honorable among all, and the bed undefiled" (Hebrews 13:4, NKJV). Sex is the one activity that makes your marriage different than any other relationship you have. It bonds you and helps two people to become one, which is the goal. As the Bible tells us, "Therefore shall a man leave his father and his mother, and shall cleave unto his wife; and they shall become one flesh" (Genesis 2:24, KJV). Neglecting this area of your relationship is not only unhealthy, it can be dangerous. God smiles on your sexual relationship with your spouse, and He created it with the purpose of developing an unbreakable bond between the two of you.

THE CHALLENGE

This week's challenge is to do something extra special to remind the two of you why you're together. Plan an extravagant or extra silly date night, have a celebration of some sort, or just spend an entire day together in your pajamas eating and watching old movies.

Whatever is special to you, *do it*!

Finally, find ways to be intimate this week. This does not necessarily mean having sex, but it does mean working your way up to that as the grand finale. Get close, touch, and hold one another as much as possible in order to get to the point where you both desire an intimate encounter. When that's the case, have a wonderful evening. The purpose in all of this is: Make it last forever.

VERSE TO REMEMBER

"Then they are no longer two but one flesh"
(Mark 10:8, NKJV).

WEEK THIRTY
PEOPLE WATCHING

While shopping in a mall recently, I was touched by a man standing outside the dressing room (I was touched emotionally not physically in case you were wondering). He looked to be in his late forties and he was waiting for his wife to try on a few things. She came out in every outfit they had chosen together to meet with either his approval or objection. That wasn't so unusual, but what intrigued me was his reaction to the items he liked.

The wife was no spring chicken and this husband wasn't doing a Donald Trump (attempting to woo a woman who could be his daughter). He was obviously so in love with his wife of perhaps more than a few years that everyone could feel it. Rather than just give a nod or a disapproving shake of the head, he would say things like, "Oh, you look *beautiful* in that," or "Honey, that was made especially for you!" The wife would emerge from the dressing room in a shy, slumped over, unassuming manner, but his response to how she looked changed her attitude, facial expression, and posture.

They had two teenage daughters who were unaffected by their discourse, which made me assume his behavior was the norm. Then I had an epiphany. This man loved on and, some would say, overly

MARRIAGE CHALLENGES

affirmed his wife for so long that the girls don't know any different. Think about the expectation of excellence in marriage he has set for those two young ladies. It made me sit back and wonder, "What if every marriage was like that?" Serve your spouse more than you've served before, love more than you've loved before, and do more than you've done before. Armed with that attitude, go forth and be the world's greatest spouse.

THE CHALLENGE

Use this couple's example of love and selflessness to improve your relationship. Spend this week affirming one another. Take the time to notice and appreciate every little thing your spouse does this week. Don't forget to write in your journal what your spouse did or said, and how it made you feel. It will be nice to look back at a journal entry and be reminded of the little things your spouse does every day to make you feel special.

VERSE TO REMEMBER

"May your fountain be blessed, and may you rejoice in the wife of your youth" (Proverbs 5:18, NIV).

WEEK THIRTY-ONE
HAPPY DIVORCE-IVERSARY

The definition of a divorce-iversary is the annual celebration of the day a divorce was finalized. It is the new normal for some to celebrate divorce with such a day. I've known people who go all out, celebrating by purchasing cakes, inviting friends to party, and making light of the end of their marriage. You can be sure I have a problem with this thinking, and this so-called "celebration."

How many times have you attended an "I failed out of school party" or an "I got fired party"? These are rare because they're not worth celebrating, and neither is a divorce. I cannot see the sense behind celebrating divorce. Marriage is a sacred relationship. It requires a vow taken before God and a host of witnesses to be faithful and true to one individual. Divorce is an admittance that you are not willing or able to do the work involved in living up to that vow.

I realize divorce happens and is often for reasons beyond the control of one of the individuals involved. The reality, however, is that divorce still signifies a failure or a loss. It signifies the death of the love that was once vibrant, exciting, and overwhelming. There may be children involved, and they are probably not celebrating (even if they smile and act like they are for their parents). They will carry the effects of the divorce for the rest of their lives.

Let's just look at it from an economic point of view. The average wedding costs $29,000 and the average divorce costs $20,000. The average counseling session costs $100, the average Bible costs $20, the average church offering is $10, and pastoral counseling and relationship building with small groups or other couples are usually free. We are willing to put tons of money into the wedding and the divorce, but we often don't utilize these marriage-enhancing resources until it is too late.

Here is my list for divorce-proofing your marriage.

1. Get counseling early and often. Premarital counseling and mentorship are essential. You need someone who will help you address the difficult questions and issues that you as a couple never imagined you would have to face. Most couples wait until they're on the verge of divorce before they seek counseling. Rather than wait until counsel is a last resort, why not be proactive and sit down with an impartial third party on a regular basis? My husband and I do what he terms a *marriage tune up* once a year or so to make sure we are on the same page. This also equips us with resources and strategies to improve our relationship. Don't neglect this and don't downplay the importance of that impartial third party who can call "foul" when either of you strikes below the belt.

2. Make some married friends who value marriage. Surround your marriage with other healthy couples. Develop friendships with these couples and limit your time with singles. I know this sounds crazy, but singles have freedoms that married individuals do not. Marriage is not a prison and your independence has not come to an end. Often, the most difficult part of marriage is taking two independent individuals and having them become one. There are some compromises that must be made. Surrounding yourself with singles often creates tempting situations and unnecessary disagreements with your spouse. Other married couples understand the compromises you've made, but also see the benefit these compromises afford you.

Couple's Bible studies or marriage support groups are great

ways to develop relationships with other marrieds. Hold a monthly (bi-monthly or even annual) activity for couples to do together. It provides mature relationships with other like-minded individuals, gives the ladies girl-time and the men guy-time, and allows you to have fun and grow together as a couple, rather than apart.

3. Get with God. Allow God to be the head of your life and your marriage. Read your Bible together and apart. Pray together as often as possible. Consider joining a Bible study or taking classes together to increase your biblical knowledge as a team. The most important factor in a marriage is the God factor. Let Him take control, and be willing to trust God in all decisions and disagreements. Putting God first reminds you that you are not in control.

THE CHALLENGE

This week, do some research. Find a good counselor or a marriage group of some sort. Then *join it*. No matter what you have to do, get yourself involved in something to edify your marriage *before* deciding between a counselor or divorce lawyer.

Then seek out other couples and plan or take part in some fun group activity or date night. You may even plan and hold a game night or a couple's dinner at your place. Whatever you decide, get the planning started this week.

When you come together, talk about what you came up with and get on the same page about what you are going to do. Most importantly, however, *do not argue* about your plan. This is supposed to be a positive and not negative situation. If you can't agree on one thing, then plan another or, even better, have more than one event. Imagine the legacy of love you will pour on other couples by hosting something to build your marriage, which in turn builds theirs.

VERSE TO REMEMBER

"Therefore what God has joined together, let not man separate" (Mark 10:9, NKJV).

WEEK THIRTY-TWO
SPEAKING THE LANGUAGE OF LOVE

It is said that marriage is a relationship in which each partner gives 50/50. You're supposed to give as much as you get, but in reality this seldom happens. There is always one spouse in greater need at any given moment. Is this fair? Probably not, but you signed up for it. Our society has made divorce the comfortable easy out when "he's not making me happy" or "she doesn't give me what I need." People buy into the lie that the difficult situation can't possibly be from God because God wouldn't allow anyone to be miserable. If you ever have that thought, stop for just a minute and focus on your spouse instead of yourself.

What if your focus was on making your spouse the happiest person in the world? What if every day you woke up with the goal of making your spouse smile often? What if you worked as hard at making a successful marriage as you do at creating a successful career?

How can you do this with the annoying spouse that you have? As Nike said, "Just do it!" And here is my best recommendation for how to do it: Discover your spouse's love language and speak it until you are blue in the face. If you are not familiar with this concept, it was developed by Gary Chapman in his book, *The Five Love Lan-*

guages. Here are the five love languages, and your spouse is fluent in at least one of them, so you need to "speak" it as well:

1. Acts of service. Clean out a desk, massage some shoulders, wash a car, or serve breakfast in bed, just to name a few.

2. Physical touch. Touch your partner's arm when you speak to him or her, hold hands everywhere, touch until he or she can't take it.

3. Words of affirmation. Affirm, affirm, and then affirm some more. Make him feel like a star and make her feel like a queen. Use your words to build up and not break down. Speak every compliment you can think of and don't keep any of them to yourself.

4. Receiving gifts. This isn't always the bling, or the extra expensive gifts. As Gary Chapman says, "A gift is something you can hold in your hand and say, she was thinking of me or he remembered me" (Chapman, 2004, p. 82). These gifts can be anything from a diamond ring to a flower picked on the way into the house. It's a token that takes thought but shows your spouse that you care.

5. Quality time. Chill with your boo as often as possible. They don't want a $1,000 date night, he or she only wants you, present and attentive to his or her needs. That means no cell phone, or iPad, and no book to read just in case (unless the two of you are reading together); it's just the two of you.

Learn your spouse's love language and then love away, because in reality, marriage is 100/100. You need to give all of you and your spouse should do the same. Remember, you can't force your partner to give that 100%, because all you can control is you. Most individuals develop a desire to give back when they receive, so you hope that eventually he or she will reciprocate. Giving all of you is the goal regardless of what your spouse chooses to do. Remember, this is where "happily ever after" truly begins, and what God requires.

THE CHALLENGE

As a fan of Gary Chapman, I have to plug his work here. Today your challenge is to go to www.5lovelanguages.com and take the quiz. Once you know your love language, over the course of the week write in your journal everything that fills your cup. For example, if you are a gifts person, write down the little things you consider a gift that would make you happy. If you are an acts-of-service type, do the same. Regardless of what language you speak, document the things that you love to have happen, based on that particular language.

When you come together, share your love language and your lists with your partner. You may want to add your spouse's list to your journal. Then make it your goal to speak your spouse's language as often as possible.

VERSE TO REMEMBER

"Love your enemies and pray for those who persecute you, that you may be children of your Father in Heaven" (Matthew 5:44-45, NIV).

(I know this may seem strange to include this verse, but you can never say you don't have any reason to serve and love your spouse. If it feels like your partner is your enemy right now, love him or her unconditionally!)

WEEK THIRTY-THREE
A PRAYER FOR MY HUSBAND

Sometimes I get so caught up in the cares of life that I forget to pray for the wonderful man God has provided as a blessing for me. Below, I present a list of prayer starters to help get your prayer party started. Men, forgive me that the list is for a wife praying for her husband. Please feel free to adjust these prayers and pray them for your wife.

1. Lord, bless my husband beyond that which he has capacity to receive.

2. Mold him into the man you've designed him to be. Help him walk in the authority you've given him, and in turn, fulfill his purpose by any means necessary.

3. Hide Your word in his heart that he may not sin against you. Remind him to seek You first in every area of his life and in every decision he makes for our family.

4. Teach him to love unconditionally. Help him to love this family with all his heart. Let this love build the self-esteem of our daughters and the self-worth of our sons. Let him share his love out loud without shame in order to teach us how to love.

5. Teach him to accept love. Help him to open his heart and

receive the love we have for him and, more importantly, to accept the love You have for him.

6. Bless our relationship. Help us to love one another in the good times and the bad. Help me to be the main pillar of his support structure, the ear he needs to listen, the shoulder he needs to cry on, and the cheerleader he needs to push him forth into his destiny. Remove all barriers to our relationship and build our bond even stronger.

7. Thank You in advance for all You have done and are doing. I trust You for the wonderful work You will perform in His life, and thank You for this awesome man with whom You have blessed me.

THE CHALLENGE

Spend time this week praying for your spouse every day. Pray when you wake up and when you go to bed, and if it crosses your mind through the course of the day, cover your spouse with prayer. In your journal, write down some of the things for which you prayed.

VERSE TO REMEMBER

"For the weapons of our warfare are not carnal but mighty through God to the pulling down of strongholds"
(2 Corinthians 10:4, KJV).

WEEK THIRTY-FOUR
"I DONT EVEN LIKE TALKING TO YOU."

My husband once said to me, "I don't even like talking to you!"

As usual, this was on the heels of a senseless disagreement. I admit that it wounded me so deeply that I didn't want to talk to *him* either. I realize this was childish and I needed to get over it, but it still hurt. It caused me to reflect on all the times I have said something that was impossible to take back – the damage was done. Once I said it, there was no apology that could remove the pain or lessen the sting from it, and it required a lot of repair work to overcome the damage.

Sadly, this happens in marriage on a regular basis. We can use words as weapons, then regret using every one of them, wishing a super-sized eraser could just wipe them all away. How do we avoid this? It's not easy for me to say while I am refusing to speak to anyone who "doesn't like to talk to me," but here is a list of reasons to keep in mind that may help you keep quiet.

1. **You are on the same team.** In football, the team would never purposely tackle its quarterback, regardless of all the terrible plays he may make. Why do we do this in marriage?

2. **Words often leave invisible scars.** Most of us would never

strike our spouse physically, but we strike one another with words on a regular basis. Stop it! Love overcomes hate every time.

3. Practice effective communication skills. What I neglected to share is that my husband said what he did because I regularly use sarcasm to stick it to him when he's working my nerves. Sarcasm is one of the number one ways of derailing quality communication. Read, search blogs, talk to counselors, or do whatever you can to acquire quality communication skills, because those skills can save your marriage.

4. God commands you to love one another. Although this statement alone says a mouthful, *just do it*! You married because of love, so don't forget that when times are difficult or when your spouse is getting on your last nerve. A disagreement, or as my pastor calls it "intense fellowship," should not take away from the love you have for your spouse.

This is not a guarantee that the two of you will not think or even say, "I don't even like talking to you." It is, however, a reminder to use your words to heal rather than to hurt. Keep in mind that many times your piercing words come in retaliation for something your spouse may have said or done. Taking a moment to think about this list may help you to change the words before they come out of your mouth. It's okay to get angry, but inflicting pain should never be the goal.

THE CHALLENGE

Today, research some communication skills and strategies for couples.

The site www.Familylife.com has a short-and-sweet article containing tools for effective communication. The title is "5 Communication Tools that Saved My Marriage," and it was written by Rob Flood. The nice thing is it has tangible principles you can put into practice immediately.

Another site, www.Crosswalk.com, often does marital communication pieces. Two that stand out are "How to Communicate in

Your Marriage" by Joe Beam, and "Developing Effective Communication in Marriage" by Edie Melson.

And www.ChristianityToday.com also has some helpful articles to get the communication ball rolling, such as, "How Can We Better Communicate in Our Marriage?" by Karen O'Connor and "Christian Couples: 5 Ways to Communicate Better" by Alannah Francis.

Journal your thoughts and impressions about some of these strategies and skills you ran across. When you come together this week, talk about what stood out to you and come to some level of agreement about how to put these into practice. Practice first with make-believe scenarios, then actually test it out with an issue that is about a 2 on a scale of 1-10. For example, gum cracking may be a 2. You don't want to practice with an issue higher than a 2 until you have practiced extensively in order to avoid a major blow out.

VERSE TO REMEMBER

"A new commandment I give you that you love one another; as I have loved you, that you also love one another. By this all will know that you are My disciples, if you have love for one another" (John 13:34-35, NKJV).

WEEK THIRTY-FIVE
A FAIR ONE

Back in the day, before everyone had an arsenal in their gun locker, we used to have what was termed "a fair one." A fair one is a one-on-one fight during which you promise not to use weapons, and friends and family members promise not to jump in. Although this seems barbaric, in the hood this was a healthy norm. You learned to protect yourself and in a not-so-normal way, you learned to solve problems on your own. The most important piece was there was no loss of life, and the honesty involved allowed the two fighters to either become friends or at least hold a level of respect for one another in the future.

The children of today know nothing of this practice. They come prepared to use whatever they can get their hands on, and if they begin losing, they either have family and friends or a weapon waiting behind a tree to give them that unfair advantage. Retaliation can continue for months, and the lack of integrity involved leaves kids with little respect for one another before, during, or after the fight.

This is the same state in many of our marriages. When you get into arguments, you can see your spouse morph into the ultimate villain and then your goal is to annihilate the enemy, rather than to solve the problem. What you can forget is that this is your teammate, your life partner, and the love of your life. You can be so interested in coming out with the win that you forget to come out with the relationship intact.

We are human, so it is inevitable that we will argue. We will disagree and there is nothing wrong with that. The problem comes in when our intention is to hurt rather than to heal the situation or the individual. Let's develop a plan to have "a fair one" with your spouse.

1. Make it "a fair one" by isolating the issue. When you argue (and especially when you feel like you're losing the argument), it is easy to pull up an old unsolved argument or issue that has nothing to do with the one at hand. Instead, make it "a fair one" by staying on topic. If you have to create a code word that communicates "we're getting off topic," use it. Do whatever it takes to stay focused.

2. Make it "a fair one" by not intentionally offending. When attempting to defend, we often offend. During an argument, you will be offended, but retaliation is not an option. Recognize this is your love and that some things will hurt simply out of ignorance not intention. With that in mind, make your disagreement "a fair one" by sharing with your spouse that you are hurt and then continue avoiding intentional offense.

3. Make it "a fair one" by listening more than you talk. God gave you two ears and one mouth. Needless to say, this must mean you are to listen twice as much as you talk. You may find yourself tempted to repeat your side of the problem over and over again in order to make your point, but what if you entered the situation with the intention of hearing your spouse's perspective? You know yours, but you don't know or understand why he or she does not get it.

4. Make it "a fair one" by taking the time to listen and hear your spouse's heart. Instead of planning your comeback while listening, be compassionate, loving, and understanding as you listen. I know that's a stretch when you are in the midst of "intense fellowship," but it has a way of turning a confrontation into a care-frontation.

5. Make it "a fair one" by taking a time out. If you feel the issue is too heated, find a safe word or phrase that will allow the two of you to step away for a time. Be sure to put parameters around this time out and develop the language that will allow you to come back to it when "cooler heads prevail." Remember, a week is too long and five minutes may be too short. Find something that works for the two of you. It's a good rule of thumb to address the issue within 24 hours if possible. This just keeps the enemy from being able to drive a wedge between you over an issue.

6. Make it "a fair one" by agreeing to disagree. There are certain issues the two of you will never agree on. This does not make either of you wrong, unintelligent, or bad people, it just highlights your differences. Learn to hear each other out and respect your varying perspectives, but agree to disagree while still loving one another.

7. Make it "a fair one" by taking all of your issues to God before attempting to take them to one another. Pray about whether it's an issue worthy of discussion, and then pray about how to address it in love. Before proceeding, if possible, you may want to pray together. I caution you against a manipulative request to pray. This is when you use prayer as a weapon rather than a valuable resource. Only pray with your spouse if you know you are both on the same page about prayer. Also, never shame your spouse with prayer. Pray silently if your spouse is not a fan of prayer, but don't do it to make your spouse feel like a heel.

THE CHALLENGE

Refer to these Rules of Engagement in order to create your own. Make your personal Rules of Engagement and post them in a prominent place. The next time you two are in a heated exchange, take a time out and look at the list together.

VERSE TO REMEMBER

"And just as you want men to do to you, you also do to them likewise" (Luke 6:31, KJV).

WEEK THIRTY-SIX
DATING IDEAS FOR COUPLES (50 FIRST DATES)

I love Drew Barrymore. Her story of how she overcame the excesses of a celebrity lifestyle is inspiring, and her subsequent success makes her heroic and a creative genius. Although her movie *50 First Dates* wasn't her best work, I went to see it because I am a fan. The movie's title sparked an idea in me, but first let me give you some background on the movie.

Drew has amnesia, so she does the same exact thing every day. One day, however, a handsome young man (Adam Sandler) encounters her routine and is awestruck. He strikes up a conversation and decides he would like to pursue a relationship with her. This doesn't set well with her friends and family, but his persistence pays off and, as in many movies, they live happily ever after (once they experience the conflict and work through it).

The movie got me thinking. In the puppy-love stage of our relationship, we are willing to do almost anything to please our significant other. Why should this stop once we get married? What would happen in your marriage if you were willing to do almost anything to make your spouse happy? That led me to the idea of documenting a list of 50 ideas for dates. This is the mother of all my lists! The purpose is to help you be intentional about making time for one another on a regular basis.

This list is too long to include here, so I have placed it in the Appendix for you to review. It is a guide to keep you from singing *The Thrill is Gone.* You don't have to do all of them, but the list covers one date night per week for one entire year. There is nothing special about the order in which I list them, and some are dictated by what area of the country or the world in which you live. Feel free to replace a date idea with another that's more pleasing to the two of you.

THE CHALLENGE

Your goal for this week is to plan how you will work your way up to a weekly date night. Since nothing is healthier to your marriage than spending couple time alone, focus on a schedule for the year. Use the chart in Appendix Two on page 155 to choose dates, but most importantly, pencil in some time for the two of you to have a regularly scheduled date night. Regardless of whether or not you choose a weekly or monthly date night, be sure to have a plan that you will make every effort to stick to it. Most importantly, plan a date for this week and have a great time together.

VERSE TO REMEMBER

"Love does no harm to a neighbor.
Therefore, love is the fulfillment of the law"
(Romans 13:10, NIV).

WEEK THIRTY-SEVEN
MAKE ME HAPPY

This is the age of entitlement. Young people today (and older ones, too) feel like they are entitled to many of the luxuries known to man. They dare you to try and withhold any good thing from them. Unfortunately, this is what happens in many marriages. People begin to think, "Your job is to make me happy, so get to it."

The partner never, ever receives this well. In fact, any demand in a marriage relationship seldom comes across well. There's almost no way to tell someone they *have* to do something and make them feel good about it, even if it was something they were planning to do.

In this age of microwave, no-fault divorce, it's easy to get to the place where you can think, "If I'm not happy, I'll get out. There are other fish in the sea, I can do better, He was a zero so let me go find a hero. I deserve better." The rationalization for your selfishness can go on and on. Instead of exercising your right to the easy way out, what if you decided to stick it out and make it work?

It's interesting that arranged marriages, which are customary in some cultures, actually outlast marriages of choice. The global divorce rate for arranged marriages is only four percent. I got some tips from a friend whose parents had an arranged marriage that is now in its fiftieth year. She said the key to their success was that they had to make it work, so they learned to fall in love over and over again. More importantly, they got to know each other before falling in love (and after they got married), mainly because they had no choice.

If that's the case with arranged marriages, why don't those of us who get the opportunity to choose our mate also choose to make it work? Why don't we choose to fall in love over and over again? That would be a novel but effective way to live.

I have an idea if you are struggling to love or even like your mate, it will take some sacrifice on your part. Even then, it may not bring the return you expect, but it will definitely pay off in the long run. To get your marriage back on track, you are going to play a game, and the game is called "Make Me Happy" (thanks Ted and Tonya for the idea), and there is only one rule: Do everything in your power to make your spouse happy every day.

That's it! The ultimate goal is to make your spouse happy through little acts of service as often as possible. Ted and Tonya compete to make coffee and serve it to each other the way he or she likes it. They compete to warm up the car, make breakfast in bed, or massage their spouse's feet without being asked. The list goes on and on.

This will require great attention to detail. You'll be forced to learn your spouse's favorite things. You'll have to work to discover your spouse's likes and dislikes. You'll have to be intentional at making their day a special one. Can you agree that serving often feels better than receiving? This is the intended outcome. Serving your spouse will make you feel good, and the added benefit is that your partner gets so overwhelmed and overjoyed by your service that he or she serves in return.

There is one caution: Never tell your spouse what you are doing to make him or her happy, or use what you did in an argument or as a bargaining chip. Either motivation negates the positive energy that went into trying to make your spouse happy. It may take some time for your spouse to notice all of the things you are doing for him (or her), but never tell.

Have you ever had someone give you a gift and then remind you they gave you that gift every time you saw them? That is what telling your spouse what you did feels like to him or her. On the flip side, never tell your spouse what they need to do for you unless asked. When you do that, it comes across like the attitude of the entitled youth of this current generation, and it puts a bad taste in the mouth of your spouse. It also comes across as nagging rather than asking.

Make sure every now and then that you ask what you can do to make your spouse happy. You can assume you know when in actuality you may be way off. You buy an expensive gift when all she wanted was a back rub, so asking is key to knowing. It gives your spouse the opportunity to share without feeling like a nag, and it helps you get in tune with him or her.

The exciting thing is that a little effort will breathe life into your marriage. The saying goes, "happy wife, happy life" and one that I made up, "happy hubby makes life bubbly." (Don't judge my corny sayings.) Spending your life making your spouse happy is the greatest service you will ever render to your family and to your marriage relationship.

THE CHALLENGE

This week, look back to some of your spouse's likes and dislikes. Take the time to do something your spouse truly enjoys every day. These can be little things like making his coffee or running her bath, just be sure to do something every day. When you come together for your weekly meeting, talk about how it made you feel to be focused on service all week. Also, talk about what you would like to continue doing on a regular basis.

VERSE TO REMEMBER

"For even the Son of Man did not come to be served, but to serve, and to give his life as a ransom for many" (Mark 10:45, NIV).

WEEK THIRTY-EIGHT
STICKS AND STONES

Sometimes couples get so comfortable with one another that they forget to share kind words or to speak the truth in love. Many an argument could be prevented if only we would think before we speak. I've often heard the saying, "It's not what you said (I'm sure you can finish it), it's how you said it." The way something was said is the point of contention in the disagreement.

We want and need our spousal relationship to be the most intimate relationship we have, so we can be vulnerable, open, and our true selves. This does not, however, give either partner a license for rudeness. My husband is my best friend, but that doesn't mean he no longer has feelings and has to accept whatever I want to say, no matter how I choose to deliver it. Here is an example of almost the exact same thing being said, but in two different ways:

"Why don't you just shut up?" or "I'm uncomfortable with this conversation right now. Would you mind giving me some time to calm down so we can communicate about it more effectively?" Can you see the difference?

You may think the latter statement does not sound like you at all. What's more, you could *never* hear yourself speaking that calmly and maturely. Imagine the kind of marriage you would have if both of you respected one another to that extent. Sheldon and I have not quite reached that level of disciplined verbal maturity, and we may never reach it. The most important thing is that we are constantly working to improve. We are learning to think about what we say before we say it, and to consider how what we are thinking can best be expressed. What we're saying and *how* we're saying it often have drastically different meanings to the sender and the receiver.

We are also practicing how to say, "What I hear you saying is... Is that what you meant?"

What a major difference a simple behavior like that can make. Many times we have had a negative interpretation of what one of us has said based on what we *think* we heard and not necessarily on what was actually said. For example, I know Sheldon and I have different accumulation-of-stuff styles. He is military in every sense of the word. He feels less is more while I am a pack rat who realizes the only way to have more is to actually get more.

When he says something about not being able to find an item, I remember all the years during which we would tear each other down on purpose. When he complains about not being able to find something, I hear him saying, "Why won't you just clean up all of this crap? I don't understand why you refuse to clean it up? What's wrong with you?" Despite the fact that he never said any of that, I read into his words another meaning behind his statement that he never intended.

After I think I heard what he didn't say, I got annoyed and my response was just short of angry and hostile – but not much short. This in turn caused his response to be terse and the cycle began. We could have easily nipped this whole issue in the bud by asking if what I heard was what he was saying. Many times I "read his mind" by saying to myself, "Even if I ask him, he'll never tell me what he really wants to say, but I know what is really on his mind."

It took many years and several good counselors for me to realize I was doing all of this and was in essence weakening my marriage.

Now I'm armed with the tools to communicate more effectively, with God's help.

Here is a summary list of this week's thoughts (I was wondering how I was going to sneak in a list).

1. Think before you speak because your spouse is human and can experience pain, even from, *especially* from you.
2. It's not *what* you say, it's *how* you say it.
3. Ask your partner if what you are hearing is what he or she is actually saying.
4. Trust that your partner's response is honest.

Your spouse is the love of your life and your goal in life is to make him or her feel loved at all times. You should feel free to speak the truth, but you should always do so in love.

THE CHALLENGE

This week, practice good communication using the strategies mentioned above. Much like you did in Week 34, find an issue that is approximately a 2 on the emotionally-charged scale of 1-10. Use this issue to practice communicating while asking for clarity. Use this statement: "What I hear you saying is... is that what you meant?" Then allow your spouse to respond with the goal of gaining understanding. In the same vein, switch places and do it again. The more you practice with less serious, less volatile issues, the easier it will be to use these strategies when the issue is more serious. That being said, practice as often as possible.

VERSE TO REMEMBER

"A soft answer turns away wrath,
but a harsh word stirs up anger"
(Proverbs 15:1, KJV).

WEEK THIRTY-NINE
LOOSE LIPS SINK SHIPS – AND MARRIAGES

Sometimes too many people are permitted to speak into your relationship. Have you been guilty of going to family or friends to vent and get a shoulder to cry on when your marriage was experiencing trouble? Maybe you shared some of the unpleasant traits and habits of your spouse in order to win people to your point of view. When you get back to a good place with your Boo, however, all the friends and family can see is the no good bum you told them about when you two were on the outs.

It is difficult not to have anyone to talk to when you and your spouse are in a bad place, but it may be necessary.

This example is exactly what many friends and family are experiencing. When we are happy in our relationships, we want them to be happy with and for us, but when we're sad or angry, we want them to share in the disdain for our spouse. The bad part is because they (friends and family) love us and only want great things for us, they want your spouse to hit the road or in the words of Martin Lawrence, "Get to steppin" once they hurt you even though you're falling back in love.

Since you were the one who vowed to love and cherish this

person for life (not the outsiders), you need to keep them out of your arguments and issues. It only gives them permission to comment on matters in your relationship that in most cases are none of their business. It's also not fair to your spouse or the friends and family you have involved. Of course, it's much easier to get through hard times with supportive friends, but those friends don't live in your house and they're not in your relationship. Be careful what you share with people because it could come back to bite you when you least expect or want it.

For your marriage to work, you must see it as the two of you going it alone against all that the world will throw at you. So you don't go running to your family with your problems, here are some things to consider that will prevent that from happening.

1. Seek godly counsel. This should only be from a counselor or some other individual who is legally bound to confidentiality.

2. Learn communication techniques. You need strategies that will help you tell your spouse about all the issues you would otherwise share with others. You can learn these techniques from books, Internet sites designed for spousal unity, and blogs that speak to positive marital relationships.

3. Join a couples group. Find a couples small group that meets in a church and allows you to share in the miseries and successes of other couples while being able to be candid about your own. Be sure this is a group bound by Scripture and confidentiality. If there isn't a group, consider starting one.

4. Identify a mentor couple. This should be a couple with more time invested in marriage than you, who have a "successful" marriage. I placed successful in quotes because you need to develop the criteria for that term. Successful doesn't just mean they're still together just holding on until one of them dies. Their relationship needs to have some substance to it. Also, recognize you may attach yourself to a couple that seems like a successful couple until you get closer and begin to see their wrinkles and flaws. Be choosy in the selection process.

THE CHALLENGE

Devise an action plan for times when you are in a season of "intense fellowship." All couples will argue and disagree, but you need an outlet when the issues are too much for you to bear alone. This person or couple could be a counselor, mentor couple, or mutually-agreeable friend(s). The key is that your disagreement cannot go any farther than that person or couple unless you both mutually agree to take it there. There can be no sister circles or man gang days where you sit and bash your spouse, because the friends and family don't know how to recover from the information when you decide to work on the relationship.

Also, decide how much you should share with this outside source. Should this include the details, or do you just share that you were upset and need a shoulder to cry on or someone to whom you can vent? If this information of who the go-to-person is can be discussed when the two of you are in a good place, it allows you to develop a plan of action with a level head before intense times come.

Be sure to discuss and agree on people you *never* want involved in your relationship. This list, by the way, should often include parents. It's difficult for your parents to forgive when they know about issues in your marriage. Although I've said this before, it bears repeating: When you and your spouse are deciding to forgive and forget, it is difficult for parents to do the same. The best way to deal with this is not to involve them in the intimate details of your arguments and issues so they can simply see both of you as their children.

VERSE TO REMEMBER

"Again, truly I tell you that if two of you on earth agree about anything they ask for, it will be done for them by my Father in heaven. For where two or three gather in my name, there am I with them" (Matthew 18:19, NIV).

WEEK FORTY
YOURS, MINE AND OURS

Although the divorce rate has decreased over time, it still hovers around the 40%-50% rate for first-time marriages and much higher for multiple marriages, which is alarming.

The fact of the matter is that divorce is still occurring, which means the blended family will become inevitable for many. The blended family is the mixing of children from previous marriage(s) with the new spouse, thereby creating a new family system. When couples are in love with one another, there is often an expectation for everything to work smoothly, something akin to, "I love her so my kids will definitely love her." The problem is many other dynamics of merging two families are often overlooked:

1. The previous spouse may not be a fan of someone he or she doesn't know spending an extensive amount of time around the child(ren).
2. The children were often against their parent's divorce. Even in abusive and conflicted relationships, the kids often prefer having their parents together, so they may resent the new spouse.
3. The children and the new spouse or the new spouse's chil-

dren may not get along.

There are many other reasons why blended families struggle, but those three are perhaps the major ones. The list below is in no particular order, but contains some ideas of how to get your blended family to a place of health.

1. The two adults should talk about your parenting skills, norms, and expectations *before* getting married. Discuss your non-negotiables. Also, talk about where you are willing to budge and negotiate with one another where discipline and expectations are concerned.

2. Share down time together. Bring all the children together and have movie nights, game nights, and any other activities that allow all of you to be yourself. There is no reason why you can't do this before you are married. The sooner you start the blending process, the better.

3. Develop family traditions and norms. It is important to establish your family as a unit. Develop your own family traditions that only you do together. For example, a secret family handshake that only you are part of. It adds to the bond only the blended family has together. Cooking breakfast for dinner on Saturdays, making up house rules for a game together, or having an annual, monthly or weekly celebration of some sort are also possible ideas. All of you should decide when and how it is celebrated, but the key is that only your blended family participates.

4. Talk about the tough stuff. Have family meetings where you are able to express the good, the bad, and the ugly. Use the feeling wheel (a tool with various emotions on it, which you will find in the Appendix) so everyone has access to or can describe as many emotions as possible. There should be ground rules, but no judgment rendered while things are being discussed. Allow the children to express themselves with no fear of punishment.

5. Become aware of the double standard. If you find yourself leaning toward favoring your own child for whatever reason, begin to analyze whether or not your motives are pure. Avoid justifying the choice, but rather analyze it to see if there are any underlying emotions.

6. Be patient with the new additions to the family. Remember, for them you are the addition and not the other way around. Allow stepchildren to grow into a relationship with you without forcing it to happen.

7. Never force the children to get along. Help to develop the relationship by doing things together (playing games, building puzzles, coloring, etc.), but be patient.

8. Respect one another and establish this rule in the house for everyone. Be sure to show respect even when it feels as if you're not receiving it. Do not allow a child to disrespect you as an adult. Consider the pain the child is in and try to see the root cause of the things the child does and says.

9. Have fun growing as a blended family. Don't neglect having fun as a family. Learn to enjoy one another's company and develop things to do as a family.

10. Don't forget that there is another mother or father probably involved in the lives of some of the children in this blended relationship. I won't go into the ground rules for that, but you need to think through that and get some help with that delicate situation.

THE CHALLENGE

Although this week's focus is on blended families, set aside time for some of the activities above regardless of whether or not you are in a blended family. Get together as a couple and talk about your parenting styles. Be real with one another and come to a consensus on some things you will and will not do as parents, even if you have no children. If you are in a blended family already, it's never too late to start to apply some of the ideas listed above. Get busy this week doing just that.

Prioritize time to be together as a family doing something fun, educational, or spiritual. Develop a family meeting time when everyone can address issues in a safe forum. Finally, stress the importance of and model respecting one another.

VERSE TO REMEMBER

"But above all these things put on love, which is the bond of perfection" (Colossians 3:14, NIV).

WEEK FORTY-ONE
SEX STARTS IN THE KITCHEN

Marriage and sex are touchy (pardon the pun) because there are so many factors that affect a couple's ability to have sex, at least quality sex, which is pleasing for both spouses. Kids, work, responsibilities, family issues, and interpersonal offenses are a few issues that can prevent couples from enjoying one another in the way God intended. I don't have a magic wand or an easy solution for these issues, but I do know that in my marriage it's much easier for me to be interested in sex when I've been wooed over the course of the day than it is to jump in and perform at the drop of a hat.

Men, the following message is for you, and I apologize in advance if you consider me sexist. If you know you want to have an evening of enjoying your wife in the bedroom, it will take preparation. No woman wants to jump into an intimate place after working all day, dealing with screaming babies, being told how dirty the house is, or how bad her food tastes. She is your spouse but she's also a human being, not a robot. Insults never work if you are trying to woo her. I can guarantee you a life of cold showers if you feel that your constant insults are helping her grow into a better person. I know it's difficult to deal with unmet needs in a kind and loving way, but you have to make the effort.

Husbands, if you don't know what to do, here is an important ground rule to follow: Make her feel like the queen of your castle and she will be more apt to make you feel like the king of the bedroom quite regularly.

The kitchen, being where many people start their day, is a great place for your romantic preparation to begin. Hug, kiss, and touch early and often, since touching is a prerequisite for intimacy. If your spouse is the primary chef or preparer in the morning, begin to help out. Ease the load of making lunches, or starting the coffee, or whatever goes on in your house. Always leave with loving words and a touch. This could be anything from "I love you" to an awesome passionate kiss (or a peck if you know your spouse isn't the passionate-kiss type). I know some couples who have their own saying or a special love pat that is reserved only for the two of them. You'd be surprised how much a secret shake, love tap, or nickname bonds you.

Throughout the day, be sure to send some type of "I love you" message, text, or better yet, a few of them. Make her feel beautiful and stress the fact that you can't live without her (or at least you never want to). I heard a man say, "I don't want to give her so many compliments that her head gets too big." I double dog dare you to try it.

Society beats women up so much by telling them they're too fat, too skinny, too tall, too short, not nice enough, not assertive enough, and the list goes on and on. Women fight a daily battle of not being enough of anything. If you think a compliment every now and again will make her become some conceited, pompous jerk, think again. Your compliments will balance her feelings of inadequacy and ground and equip her to go out into the harsh world again. She needs to hear good things so that the enemy is not able to twist and manipulate her into focusing on everything she's not. When in doubt, let *every* compliment out.

When a woman feels loved, she is better able to love. When a woman loves with all she's got, watch out. God designed her eyes to be for her man, so when she feels loved and wanted, she will almost always smother you with affection. The flip side is also true. Please don't take these tips and use them only for your benefit. When a woman feels manipulated, she becomes guarded and once again, it's off to the cold showers.

The moral of this story is to love your wife with all your heart, understand her needs, and be her biggest, most vocal cheerleader. In turn, she will love, honor, and serve you as the king of your castle. Always remember that sex starts in the kitchen, not the bedroom.

THE CHALLENGE

This week's challenge is to test the theory that sex starts in the kitchen. Take the entire week and smother one another with affection. Start first thing in the morning. Spend the day intimately touching one another. This could be in the form of actual physical touch or a sweet loving text or note that makes your spouse feel like a rock star. Finally, pour on the compliments this week. Don't make up a shallow saying just to fulfill this challenge, but rather think long and hard and share those sincere things you want your spouse to know.

VERSE TO REMEMBER

"Husbands, love your wives, even as Christ also loved the church, and gave himself for it" (Ephesians 5:25, KJV).

WEEK FORTY-TWO
SEX STARTS IN THE KITCHEN - PART TWO

To continue our topic of sex starting in the kitchen, I'd like to focus attention on women this week. There are many things I could write here to tell a woman how to prepare her man for a sexual encounter, but in reality, the average man needs little to no coaxing when it comes to the matter of sex. I will, however, add that there are some things women can do and say to make sexual encounters more enjoyable for your spouse.

Let's go forward by first going back. I remember a television commercial from some time ago that featured a professional yet sexy woman describing her skills as a boss in the boardroom *and* the bedroom. She talked about being able to buy the bacon and cook it with excellence. She also talked about never letting her husband forget he's a man.

This commercial spoke volumes to the women who have moved into the workforce and successfully navigated what used to be the "man's world." There is absolutely nothing wrong with a woman being a professional by day, but the problem comes in when the wife gets so caught up in that world that she forgets the needs of her husband at night.

Regardless of whether you are the stay-at-home domestic engineer running the household like a well-oiled machine, or the working woman "doing it for herself," there is still a need to maintain a thriving marriage. This commercial drove home the fact that men are driven by the physical. This is not a flaw but rather a characteristic of their God-ordained design. With that in mind, there are a few things a wife can do to help her man uphold this area while helping her marriage in the process.

1. Plan chores and responsibilities to make love-making a priority. If you find yourself folding or ironing clothes at bedtime, or doing the dishes until he falls asleep, it may be time to change your routine. This could include giving some of the chores to the children if they are old enough, or putting the kids to bed a little earlier, which would necessitate eating, doing homework and bath time being earlier in order to make this happen. If you make your husband aware of the ultimate goal, I'm almost certain he will pitch right in to help.

2. Get that body right. This is not intended to be a sexist statement, because I totally understand the struggle to maintain the "perfect" figure. I'm not saying work out until you finally leave the gym with a Beyoncé body, but I am saying get healthy, and get yourself into shape. The first and most important part is the healthier you are, the better you feel. Recognize that a size 6 doesn't equate to being healthy, neither does starving yourself to fit into a societal definition of sexy. The goal is being the best you that you can be. When you're happy with you, the confidence you exude is immeasurable. Therefore, getting into shape will in most cases make your man that much more drawn to you.

3. Get dressed up on a regular basis. This doesn't mean that you don a red dress and high heels every day, but it does mean to take care of yourself. Many women got their man's attention by looking as good as possible as often as possible. This does not have to change once you're married. Be intentional about getting dressed up for him. Please understand I am not saying that you have to be a super model the minute you hear his car in the driveway, but I am asking that you put some effort into not always hanging around in a moo-moo or sweat pants.

4. Allow your body to create the physical imprint he sees when he's led to think sexually. Once again, I'll say from experience that weight gain from childbirth and stress cause the female body to go through quite a few changes. The stretch marks and various scars that cannot be removed may make you feel like you are unlovable, but regardless of what your body has been through, your man wants to see it. He wants to see it in as little as possible, and he wants to see it as often as possible. The more comfortable you become with the skin you're in, the sexier you will be. One of the many issues with pornography is it leaves a visual imprint on the brain. This imprint is what creates the desire to see more and eventually develops a thirst that is somewhat unquenchable. In marriage, however, you can combat this imprint by allowing your husband to see your naked or scantily-clad body regularly, so that this is the imprint that dominates his psyche. He loves you and he wants to see all of you.

5. Keep Extra Strength Tylenol in stock. The goal is to have less headaches in order to enjoy your husband more. The sacrifice you make at times will allow him to love you all the more.

Please take this for what it is, which are helpful hints to enable you to steam up the bedroom in order to improve your relationship. The only purpose is to ensure that sex starts in the kitchen for the husband as well as the wife.

THE CHALLENGE

This week's challenge is to be as sexual as possible. It's time to buy something new or try something new (or both). A good goal is to have sex each evening this week. Remember, this is the week to celebrate your husband. As I wrote earlier, women give sex to get affection while men give affection to get sex. This being the case, and since the women got all the affection they could possibly want last week, this week give all the sex you possibly can.

VERSES TO REMEMBER

"Do not withhold good from those to whom it is due, when it is in your power to do it" (Proverbs 3:27, NASB).

"And the man and his wife were both naked and unashamed" (Genesis 2:25, NASB).

WEEK FORTY-THREE
THE POWER OF PORN

Everyone has heard the term in the world of advertising, "sex sells." Most of us don't see the connection between a bikini-clad woman in a car commercial and buying a car, but it must work. In reality, "sex sells" is much more pervasive than in advertising. Sex sells the innocence of the young people involved, it sells the virtue of women forced to turn to it for an income, and it sells the integrity of the men (and women) who quickly become addicted to gawking at it on a regular basis.

It is the new form of selling your soul to the devil, because a quick look turns into hours of uninterrupted Internet searches, or thousands of dollars spent to feed a hunger that can never be satisfied.

There was a time when people were ashamed to look at pornography. Porn was hidden in basements and garages, or in the bottom of what looked like a garbage can, so that no one would know the addiction with which the individual was battling. There was a time when a boy would find his father's secret stash and bring it to school. The boys would be lost in a glazed-over stare, not knowing what it was, but knowing that it was something naughty that they should not have. They still had the wherewithal to hide it lest anyone see it and take it away.

In this day and age of full disclosure and exposure, we no longer experience shame, or as my pastor says, "We can no longer blush." When we don't blush, we have no boundaries. We don't realize when we've gone too far, and in the 21st century, we have gone too far. I live in a city where we have a strip club half a block away from a middle school. The students have to pass this club to get to public transportation, and two of the school busses have to park directly in front of this club while the students board. I can't imagine what these children have been exposed to by standing outside the door of that club for the fifteen minutes or so it takes to board the bus every day. The problem is this club and the perversion it takes to maintain it are becoming normalized for these children at this early age. They don't stand a chance against this trick of the enemy.

We live in an age where most people feel there is nothing wrong with pornography. We see soft porn on commercials, billboards, magazine racks, and almost everywhere we turn. We also feel it's not hurting anyone. There are so many negative effects connected to porn, that I am not going to try to list them. I will, however, make an attempt to identify the impact that porn has on a marriage.

1. Pornography causes the viewer to shape or fashion a fantasy sexual man or woman. This fantasy becomes an unrealistic standard by which the partner begins to judge the spouse. Porn performers are paid to show their bodies to the world, so they spend a good portion of their life in the gym or with plastic surgeons trying to perfect every part of their body. The expectation that your wife or husband should look like one of these performers is unfair and virtually impossible to fulfill. The average dress size is between 14-16. The average male waist line is 42 inches. The average porn star weighs 115 lbs. and wears a size 0-2. The male stars have a 32-inch waist. I share those statistics only to stress the unrealistic fantasy porn stars create.

2. We develop sexual expectations based upon what occurred in a make believe movie. Pornography is designed to turn people on sexually. It initially imitated what happened in the bedroom, but has evolved into some odd and uncomfortable, and at times virtually impossible, movements and positions designed to stimulate those who have deadened their impulses by regular porn viewing and must be shocked in order to be turned on. This places an expectation on a spouse to carry out some of these uncomfortable and shocking movements that no longer bring pleasure but instead make the spouse feel inferior to the porn star, or inferior as a man or woman, unable to please his or her partner.

3. Porn breeds insecurity in your spouse. Your spouse will feel as if he or she is constantly compared to someone else. Every time you look on another woman or man with lust, it degrades the self-worth and sensuality of your spouse. When your head no longer turns for your spouse, it degrades him or her as well. Your partner feels like there is a competition, and since the other man or woman is not real, it's a competition your partner can *never* win. The woman on the screen never talks back, rarely has an opinion, and is always ready to perform. It's all unreal!

4. Finally, pornography is sin. Pornography leads to lust and lust is sin. It is the enemy's plot to destroy and mar the sexual act between a married man and a woman, which God created as good. Anything that perverts that is to be avoided like Ebola or some other modern day plague.

One the next pages are a few of the passages that address sexual immorality and lust, but there are many more. The enemy does not allow anyone to stop at simply looking at porn. He always pushes a little more until the addicted find themselves in situations they would never have thought possible. They find themselves defending their decisions to delve into areas they know are inappropriate and that endanger their marriage. Porn is the gateway to much more, and avoiding it at all costs is the only way to truly survive this evil that's in your face all the time.

THE CHALLENGE

This week is the opportunity to go a little deeper in your walk with Christ. If you have found yourself involved in some level of pornography or lust, take the time to repent for the sin. Sincerely go to God with this issue with the intention of receiving His help to end this struggle. After repenting, seek out help in the form of a support group, a counselor, a pastor, or an online resource like "Covenant Eyes."

If you are not involved in any pornography use or addiction, this week take the time to pray for the strength to avoid it at all costs. Don't forget to pray for your spouse as well. When you complete this prayer, write a pledge in your journal that you will resist the temptation to resort to pornography. With this pledge, write the people who will hold you accountable to this pledge. When temptation comes, remember this pledge and call on the people you wrote down.

There are also various websites designed to help in this fight, such as www.nopornpledge.com and www.antipornography.org and www.fightthenewdrug.org. They are just a few designed to help in the struggle and to create a large network of like-minded individuals who understand the negative repercussions of pornography. Take some time to go through their material and bookmark those things that interest you. It may even be helpful to do this with your spouse.

When the two of you come together, pray for one another and against this problem that kills the intimacy in marriages.

VERSES TO REMEMBER

"Flee from sexual immorality. All other sins a person commits are outside the body, but whoever sins sexually, sins against their own body. Do you not know that your bodies are temples of the Holy Spirit, who is in you, whom you have received from God? You are not your own; you were bought at a price. Therefore, honor God with your bodies" (1 Corinthians 6:18-20, NIV).

"But I tell you that anyone who looks at a woman lustfully has already committed adultery with her in his heart" (Matthew 5:28, NIV).

"Marriage should be honored by all, and the marriage bed kept pure, for God will judge the adulterer and all the sexually immoral" (Hebrews 13:4, NIV).

"Dear friends, I urge you, as foreigners and exiles, to abstain from sinful desires, which wage war against your soul" (1 Peter 2:11, NIV).

"But each person is tempted when they are dragged away by their own evil desire and enticed. Then, after desire has conceived, it gives birth to sin; and sin, when it is full-grown, gives birth to death" (James 1:14-15, NIV).

Put on the full armor of God, so that you can take your stand against the devil's schemes. For our struggle is not against flesh and blood, but against the rulers, against the authorities, against the powers of this dark world and against the spiritual forces of evil in the heavenly realms. Therefore, put on the full armor of God, so that when the day of evil comes, you may be able to stand your ground, and after you have done everything, to stand. Stand firm then, with the belt of truth buckled around your waist, with the breastplate of righteousness in place, and with your feet fitted with the readiness that comes from the gospel of peace. In addition to all this, take up the shield of faith, with which you can extinguish all the flaming arrows of the evil one. Take the helmet of salvation and the sword of the Spirit, which is the word of God (Ephesians 6:11-17, NIV).

WEEK FORTY-FOUR
TAKING ONE FOR THE TEAM

Anyone who has ever been involved in sports will know what it means to take one for the team. This can mean anything from allowing someone else to take the winning shot to riding the bench while another player gets a chance. That player may not be the best at the position, but with a chance, he or she can develop into something great. So the player not playing makes a sacrifice for the good of the team. This concept can also apply to marriage.

I often remind married couples that they are the ultimate teammates. You are in it to win it and you can't allow anyone to take on your marriage and win. This is much easier said than done, especially when your teammate is a ball hog. It's difficult to want to sacrifice your time for someone else to shine when they don't seem willing to do the same. With enough love and vision, however, you can change this attitude.

Enough with the analogies, let's get real. When your spouse is offending you in public, it's difficult to turn the other cheek and allow him or her to continue. Taking one for the team means seeing things from your spouse's point of view. It's difficult but can be beneficial, if you're both willing to learn from it. Being able to recognize that your spouse offending you in public is possibly because his supervisor spent the day fussing at him, and he is struggling to learn how not to bring his work home or into your relationship. You realize that your wife spent her day running after zealous, energetic toddlers, and therefore doesn't have the energy to meet your needs. That is taking one for the team, and it requires humility and maturity.

What would happen if instead of snapping back at your spouse, your response was, "Honey it sounds like you had a rough day at work. Would you like to talk about it? I promise I'll just listen and not offer an opinion unless you want me to." Or, "I can see you have had a rough day, Babe. Let me take the kids for a ride so you can catch a nap!"

Taking one for the team is sensing how your spouse feels as he or she comes home and, instead of being offended by his or her exhaustion or irritation, you jump in to do the dishes or massage a back or tired feet. If you haven't been doing this in the past, your partner may be in shock and question your motives, but eventually this norm will remind your spouse why you got married and may encourage him or her to find ways to take one for the team as well.

You and your spouse are the perfect pair and the ultimate team, and you must work to create the conditions for the agreement needed for God to be in your midst. Don't allow the enemy and any of his schemes to get in and destroy what you have together. Pray for your team on a daily basis and allow God to take you to new heights of happiness, satisfaction, and winning by being willing to take one for the team every now and then.

THE CHALLENGE

My pastor often uses the phrase, "hurt people hurt people." This week, purposely attempt to see things from your spouse's perspective. When he or she is sharp or a little testy, instead of taking it personally, begin to imagine what may have happened over the course of the day to elicit this reaction. Keep your feelings at bay and try to be there for your spouse this week. As you practice this from this week on, it will make it easier to implement this practice on a regular basis.

> ## VERSE TO REMEMBER
>
> "For where two or three are gathered together in my Name, there am I in the midst of them" (Matthew 18:20, KJV).

WEEK FORTY-FIVE
I LOVE YOU BUT I DON'T LIKE YOU

I often tell people that marriage is a wonderful thing because it's a true statement. Marriage provides companionship, keeps one from loneliness, and makes life a more enjoyable experience, at least for some.

I've heard women say from time to time, "I love him but I don't like him." The first question I never ask but always think is, "Why in the world would you marry someone you don't like?" I realize now the answer develops from years of unresolved issues. Couples are caught up in puppy love before the wedding, and they often forget to deal with the real stuff before and especially after the ceremony. It still baffles me, however, that anyone would commit to a life together and be willing to be miserable from that day forward.

Many couples fall head over heels in love and forget to use their head to figure out if they are truly in love, in lust, or looking for a cure to their loneliness. Hindsight creates a 20/20 vision on the past, which can cause people to say after ten years of marriage, "I realize now I only married her because I was tired of being alone," or "He was the first one to really show an interest in me." It makes me wonder what would have happened if they had recognized that truth before saying "I do"? They would have saved a lot of time, pain, and money.

That begs the question: "How do you grow to learn to *like* your spouse?" I can't answer that for you, but I can give you some tips on how to get the party started, and of course I will do so through a list.

1. Get to know one another. Play games like 20 Questions that I recommended in week 11. Find out what your spouse likes, what he hates, her favorite color, his favorite car, her dreams, and even his nightmares. Get to know your spouse so well that no one can come between you. Keep in mind that all that can change with age, so you have to play 20 Questions regularly.

For example, I hated Brussel sprouts all my life. I thought they were nasty balls of slime created to torture young children everywhere. When I grew up and participated in a Daniel fast, it opened my eyes to the wonderful refreshing taste of a tiny little cabbage designed to provide health and nutrition. It would have been easy for my husband to continue to think I hated those sprouts, but we took the time to update one another on my new like. That's a simple example of how we share our lives together by having regular talking points when we update one another about our likes and dislikes, and that allows us to grow together.

2. Talk often and openly. Share everything you can think of. Share with your spouse all the stuff you would normally reserve for your best friend or confidante. Remember woman, your man is not a woman, so be careful about overloading him with details like, "Her Juicy Couture bracelet took my breath away." Remember man, spare your woman from statements like, "The catalytic converter caused the a-frame to go." When you get to know your spouse, you'll begin to recognize how to talk to your spouse.

But whatever you do, *never* stop talking. The talk is the fuel and lubricant for companionship. It fulfills the lonely space that can grow when you aren't able to communicate with people on a regular basis. What is the purpose of living with someone to whom you never talk?

3. Have fun together. I am going to return to this topic in upcoming weeks, but we have already discussed some of the ideas I have on it. Fun should be part of all life, especially the life with the one you love.

4. Forgive. Forgive your spouse for the thing she did, the thing he said, the way she looked at you, the way he talked to you in public. The best way to save a marriage is to forgive every day, all day long. It will revolutionize your marriage. I always refer back to my friend Joy's statement, "I enter every situation assuming my husband has my best interest at heart." When she filters all that her husband Seth says and does through that perspective, she's able to forgive the hurt he may cause her (often unknowingly and definitely not purposely). Those of us with a clogged filter see our spouse as the enemy and imagine that everything he or she does is another attempt at retaliation. Begin to see things from Joy's perspective.

For example, my husband and I were walking in a dangerous area of Jamaica. He became leery about some men following us and rather than speaking with kind words, his awareness and police training kicked in and he snarled orders at me. I was immediately offended and wouldn't talk to him for a while after that. He was later able to explain what he was doing, and I was able to see his objective was to keep me safe. I could have held on to my feelings of frustration and hurt, but instead decided to forgive, knowing his intentions were pure. It just came wrapped in fear for my life and the need to protect me. He couldn't stop to find loving and healing words; he needed quick lifesaving words and a powerful tone. Stop seeing your spouse as the enemy and begin seeing him or her as the ultimate teammate.

5. Read the book, *The Five Love Languages.* If you've never read it, I urge you to do so. It is a quick read and will bless your life and your marriage. If you've read it before, take the time to read it again (preferably with your spouse). It will remind you of where your focus needs to be for your spouse. Whether or not he or she reads it with you, it will help your relationship as you learn to serve

MARRIAGE CHALLENGES

your spouse's highest-priority needs and hopefully watch your partner reciprocate.

THE CHALLENGE

This is another talking week. Over the course of the week, write in your journal everything you wish the two of you had time to talk about. This could be anything from the new budget you need to create, or the next hairstyle you would like to try, or the new car you would like to buy. When you come together, take your list with you and share from your heart. My friends Mike and Maxine, who have been married for more than forty years, mentioned setting up some of your favorite snacks for an activity like this. It's helpful to have something good and comforting to eat when you decide to spend uninterrupted quality time with the one you love. If the conversation flows (which is the hope), use this time to build your bond, but make sure you have your journal and that each of you gets to talk about the things you wrote down.

Most importantly, don't allow this to be the only time you do this. With life happening at warp speed, you may have to schedule in your quality time, but do not neglect the need to get to know one another. My husband often notes the transitions we've gone through in our seasons of life, from our teens, through our twenties, into thirties and now forties. We have been together through all of this and have become different people. Incorporating these quality-time touch points will allow you to get to know everything about your ever-evolving spouse, and will keep you up-to-date on the changes he or she is going through.

VERSE TO REMEMBER

"Above all, love each other deeply, because love covers over a multitude of sins" (1 Peter 4:8, NIV).

WEEK FORTY-SIX
AFFAIR-PROOF YOUR MARRIAGE

I once read that eight out of ten marriages will experience an affair, which is a staggering percentage. It isn't that surprising, I suppose, when you consider that temptation is everywhere. The Internet is a new way to connect with people of the opposite sex (and even the same sex). Travel makes "anonymous" sex possible — people meet, do the deed, and then return home as if nothing happened. We've also been inundated with the message that if your marriage doesn't make you happy, move on. We have a microwave culture that communicates everything should work within ten minutes or less, or it's not worth the effort. A successful marriage, however, requires that you resist cultural norms that feed selfish desires and instant gratification.

1. In the movie *City Slickers*, Billy Crystal said, "Women need a reason to have sex, men just need a place." That being the case, how can spouses be more in tune with one another? I am by no means suggesting that women have to give it up on demand or that men have to create a theme every time they would like to make love. I am suggesting the idea of being more receptive to the needs of your partner in this area. If women are willing to add an additional night for sex here or there, men may come away more satisfied and

gratified. On the flip side, if men will make love to the wife's mind and woo her over the course of the day, she may be more willing and able to perform when the moment is right. The key here is serving one another. The selfless act of giving in to the needs of the spouse can make all the difference in the area of sexual gratification.

2. According to *The Huffington Post* (2013), 70% of men and 30% of women access Internet porn. This article actually finds that "porn sites get more visits than Netflix, Amazon, and Twitter combined." Although the world paints this as harmless fun, the reality is that porn creates a false pretense of what sex is and should be. It turns love to lust and makes human beings nothing more than sex objects, depicting sexual interaction as a means of self-gratification. Since porn creates a lust that can never be quenched, the increased need for more perverse activities produces an uncomfortable imbalance of selfish need and satisfaction, versus the desire to please one another.

3. Another area of temptation is travel. Travel often allows the temptation to "just do it" (in the words of Nike) because no one will ever know. Hotel rooms and unfamiliar surroundings provide the secrecy needed to carry out acts some would never consider acceptable in their own home or even their own community. Even the access to private Internet porn is a temptation some would never consider giving in to when at home. You need to be hypervigilant about guarding your eyes, guarding your heart, and being accountable to someone.

4. What about honesty in temptation? Too often couples don't share their temptations because of shame (what will she think about the fact that I was attracted to that woman? What will he think that I flirted with that man?). "We have to remove the shock response whenever we have honest communication" (Stanko, 2016).

This level of open honesty is often uncomfortable for couples. It's okay to talk about being attracted to Janet Jackson, not that anyone I know feels that way (seething with sarcasm because she has for many years been the girl of my husband's dreams), but not that girl at the bus stop. We are okay with the impersonal fantasies, but those that are closer to home are difficult to discuss. This is an area I too will admit is difficult. I don't want to hear that my husband feels a certain way about someone he encounters every day, but my disdain or disapproval teaches him to keep that secret. Secrets are where the enemy does his best work. He can turn a secret into something shameful, which allows him to twist and contort it until we find ourselves in situations we didn't think were possible.

Find ways to talk about the temptations you experience on a regular basis. Getting them out in the open removes the power they have over you. It also allows you to accept the feeling and pray for one another concerning the temptation.

5. Salt-N-Pepa had a popular song in 2009 entitled *Let's Talk about Sex*. While we are talking about temptation, why not throw in a talk about sex? For some reason, this is an uncomfortable topic for many couples. Although they participate in it, many people find it difficult to talk about sex. My husband and I actually took a class where the teacher did an activity to 'desensitize' us to sexual vocabulary. In a room of approximately 100 people, we had to yell out between 15 and 20 sexual-organ/slang terms together until the words no longer made us blush. I will admit it was very uncomfortable in a class full of men and women, but the activity worked. You may want to try something silly like this with your spouse in order to break the ice.

Once you are comfortable enough to say these things with your spouse, take it a step further. Begin to talk about your sex life. Talk about things you like and the things you dislike. Talk about when and how often you would like to have sex. Talk about who initiates most and if you would like this to change. Talk about things you would like to try together and things that may be off limits (at least for now). Remember not to shame or insult your partner, but get to know the things you both want out of your sex life.

Finally, and most importantly, schedule sex. I know people believe scheduling takes all the spontaneity out of the act, but it doesn't have to be that way. In fact, if done appropriately, it can make it that much more enjoyable. If you know that every Sunday you will have sex, you can begin to plan for it. You can make it special. Send little lovey-dovey texts all day, buy accessories and lingerie, prepare special food, snacks, or decorate a particular area. You have time to make it extra special! This doesn't mean you can't have sex other days; it just means that barring a natural disaster, this is the non-negotiable (for the most part) day that you have sex.

6. Our marriage vows said we accept one another "in sickness and in health." What about pregnancies, illnesses, and other times when couples need to be vigilant to avoid temptation? These are times when temptation rears its ugly head. When a long-term illness or pregnancy occurs, many times spouses are left to go days, weeks, months, and, I'm sad to say, even years without sexual satisfaction. The fact of the matter is that when one spouse cannot perform, this in no way lessens the desire for the partner who can. It is difficult to imagine that a spouse could have an affair when their mate is ill or pregnant, but it happens on a regular basis. There must be some safeguards in place in order to avoid this.

The first safeguard is constant prayer and devotion to the Word of God. Do this in the form of a devotional or Bible-reading plan. Finding a study focused on sexual issues may be wise during this time because it will arm you with strategies to fight temptation. Second, get people around you to pray for and with you on a regular basis. Third, find an accountability partner with whom you pledge to be completely honest. Finally, have a talk with your spouse about what you are experiencing. They may have other ways of relieving your stress, or at least of sympathizing with you.

7. A most important piece to affair-proof your marriage is incorporating some level of marriage mentorship. This is that go-to couple whom you can trust with the issues you experience. Remember, the idea is to mentor and be mentored. The mentor couple for you can act as accountability partners. When you're experiencing temptation and are not yet comfortable enough to share with your spouse, use the same-sex member of this mentor couple to be your confidante. If you and your spouse have an issue you cannot resolve, this couple may be able to referee your conversation. They may also

have experienced what you're going through and have the wisdom and understanding to help you navigate it as well. Keep in mind that you are not meant to do this alone. Lean on that mentor couple and allow them to invest their time and energy into your success.

Affair-proof your marriage by working as hard as you can to be the best spouse you can be. This by no means explains the selfish nature of individuals who have affairs despite having a wonderful marriage. Only sin can explain that behavior. When it comes down to it, however, do all you can to fight off the enemy's attack on your marriage, which is a real and present danger for all of us.

THE CHALLENGE

This was a long chapter. Take some small chunks of each item and make it a priority to study and discuss. Here are some things to do while you are studying:

- Intentionally set out to please your spouse.
- Pray for one another in the area of porn or other temptations. Pray that God would guard your eyes and increase desire for one another while decreasing the desire for others.
- Plan time to talk, seek out, or actually plan a time to spend with your mentor couple, if you haven't already done so.
- Also, plan time to talk with your spouse about sex and some of the other topics touched on this week.

VERSES TO REMEMBER

"Let no corrupt word proceed out of your mouth, but what is good for necessary edification, that it may impart grace to the hearers" (Ephesians 4:29, NKJV).

"No temptation has overtaken you except what is common to mankind. And God is faithful; he will not let you be tempted beyond what you can bear. But when you are tempted, he will also provide a way out so that you can endure it" (1 Corinthians 10:13, NIV).

WEEK FORTY-SEVEN
MAKE MARRIAGE FUN

My husband and I find a way to compete over almost anything. For example, we compete to see who can be the first one to use the shower. It started as a joke, but then turned into an intense game. The need to have the first shower takes over and we will connive and plot to see who wins.

I share that to encourage you to make your marriage fun. Competition is healthy and good, and it often puts a smile on your face. You may not be smiling right away, but once the agony of defeat wanes, it can be a tradition that brings joy and creates memories. There are times when I come home, see him in his robe, but don't really notice until well into our conversation:

"Hey babe. How was your day?"

"Pretty good. How about yours?"

"Ahh it was . . . Hey, why are you in your robe?"

He's in his robe because he beat me to the shower. That moment is total victory for him. He feels vindicated for all of the nights I beat him there and rubbed it in his face. When he wins, I am motivated to get home earlier the next day and take the first shower, even if it means showering at 5 o'clock.

I realize it sounds crazy, but we have created a fun tradition that has carried down to our children. They love conspiring with one of us to make sure we win. It's silly and not important, but it builds a bond of laughter and fun that helps our family function.

Take the time to play fun games or create silly competitions that make your marriage the best relationship you have. Some ideas for this area are:

1. Inside jokes are a must. A funny word or just a word said in your times of silliness can become the trigger for uncontrollable laughter. Use these times to your advantage and remind yourself of them often. Even if it makes people look at the two of you like you're crazy, it secures your place as your spouse's best friend.

2. Play, play, play. If you are the sports type, take up a sport the two of you can participate in together. Group sports are nice, but couple sports are even better. They provide time for you as a couple while taking part in a sport you love. If you don't have one in common, try as many different activities as you can until you find one you both love. Racquetball, tennis, air hockey, or bike riding are just a few. Do whatever is fun and memorable. Shel and I found our sweet spot in Dance, Dance Revolution. Laugh if you must, but with us, DDR is real! We stretch before and after, and we play like there's a cash prize at the end. Sheldon even went as far as purchasing the real video game version because the little plastic pads are for amateurs, in our (not so) humble opinions.

3. Be spontaneous. Do something just because you think of it. Get in the car and drive. Wherever you end up is where you stay. Have a date on the living room floor. Lay out a blanket, get a basket, and eat together right there. Take time to share your dreams for the night. Do something totally out of character for the two of you. It will make for together time and the awkwardness of not doing something well will bond you with laughter.

4. Embarrass one another. This can be touchy and you must know your spouse in order for this to work. Your goal is not to offend but to make your spouse smile even if that means smiling through a red face. When a great song comes on in a supermarket, to my chagrin Sheldon breaks out in dance like he's at a nightclub. My response is to run to the next aisle as quickly as possible so as not to be associated with him. It's embarrassing but we laugh for hours after it occurs. He will also roll down the window while we're driving and whisper something like, "She farted." This infuriates me when someone is there, but sends me into uncontrollable laughter when we get away from the other motorists. Think about ways to embarrass but not demoralize your spouse, something that causes laughter not shame. Charlie Chaplin said, "A day without laughter is a day wasted." I agree. Laugh hard and laugh often but most importantly, laugh together.

THE CHALLENGE

This is another week to pull out the goofy side of your personality. Take time each day this week to purposely make your spouse laugh as hard as possible. Also, throughout the week incorporate some of the activities above. Develop a safe secret word – something that every time you hear it you both burst into laughter or that at least elicits a snicker. Play something together, or take in a sporting event you both enjoy. Do something spontaneous and find a cute way to embarrass one another.

VERSE TO REMEMBER

"Nothing is better for a man than that he should eat and drink, and that his soul should enjoy good in his labor" (Ecclesiastes 2:24, NKJV).

WEEK FORTY-EIGHT
IN SICKNESS AND IN HEALTH

My husband recently had a second surgery for a shoulder injury. Although that may sound like a minor issue to some, the reality is that there is a chance of death every time someone goes under anesthesia. For this reason, despite my trust for the Savior and knowing my husband still has work to do here, I was a little shaken during both surgeries.

These surgeries were a reminder for me to cherish the love of my life every day. It allowed me to reminisce on our good times, to think of the days when we'd get in the car and drive to see the autumn leaves changing colors. Or the times when we would run to the movies to see a flick that might not interest us but rather allowed us to be together and alone. Or the nights we would run downstairs on a cereal date, which consisted of a midnight run to the kitchen when no one else was awake to steal some private time indulging in a snack we both love.

The surgeries emphasized the importance of being there for one another, willing and able to do whatever I needed to do whenever Shel needed it. I took on the challenge of hearing him moan and groan in pain. I dealt with the crankiness that accompanies a lack of sleep, I cleaned up the messes he made, and endured the trials of rehab while encouraging and empowering him to help maintain his dignity.

"In sickness and in health" is part of our vows when we get married. We shared this vow in front of a crowd of invited guests who celebrated and shared in our big day, forgetting their true purpose was to act as witnesses to the sacred covenant we were making to one another before God. When we make that vow, we seldom think about the day we will carry our partner up the steps, or clean up the mess made on the bathroom floor (if he or she makes it to the bathroom). A debilitating injury can be life threatening as well as relationship threatening, so how can we endure through this trial?

During Shel's surgeries, I had to consider our relationship from the "in sickness" perspective for the first time. I would offer this advice from my caregiving role. Make the best of your relationship every day. Enjoy the good times (health) so that you get so wrapped up and in love that the down times (sickness) aren't such a struggle. I heard my pastor say when his wife went through a bout with cancer that he counted it an honor to take care of her. He was so in love with that woman that his service to her helped build their bond rather than tear it apart. If we could all get to this point, divorce would truly not be an option.

What I am saying is easier said than done, and Shel's injury was not ongoing or terminal. I did use his recovery period to remind myself of the wonderful traits that made me fall in love with him. You should take some time to do the same. Then think about the things that also caused your spouse to fall in love with you. Try to re-create as many of those characteristics as you can. I've been with my husband since I was fifteen years old, so some of the things that made him fall in love with me would look silly and out of character for the fully-grown woman I am now. I do recognize, however, that sometimes a little bit of out-of-character silliness does make the heart grow fonder. All I am saying is to be intentional about being lovable to your spouse whether or not he or she can or is willing to reciprocate.

THE CHALLENGE

This is another week for gratitude. Take the week thinking about and writing about some things you love that your spouse has done for you. Write about what your spouse means to you and why your relationship is so important. When you come together at the end of the week, share your list, and let him or her know how much you appreciate your relationship.

VERSE TO REMEMBER

"Love is patient, love is kind. It does not envy, it does not boast, it is not proud. It is not rude, it is not self-seeking, it is not easily angered, it keeps no record of wrongs. Love does not delight in evil but rejoices with the truth. It always protects, always trusts, always hopes, always perseveres. Love never fails"
(1 Corinthians 13:4–8, NIV).

WEEK FORTY-NINE
MARRIAGE REVIVAL

Marriage is a day-in, day-out, all-in, 100% commitment. It can be wonderful and joyous, but it can also be trying and stressful. No matter where you are in your relationship or how long you have been together, you can use a revival.

Revival in the church was known as a time of coming together to be spiritually refreshed. It gives a renewed sense of purpose, and provides inspiration and motivation for spiritual things. A church revival consists of services that are enhanced by the expectations of those who gather. Those who anxiously anticipate something spiritual are almost always rewarded.

What is a marriage revival? It is also a time of refreshing when couples come away with a renewed sense of purpose, inspiration, and motivation. In this day and age of dual-career households, a revival can be difficult to achieve, but never more needed. You must make time to be alone with one another for your marriage, or you will find that you have drifted apart before you know it.

It is easy to put your marriage on the back burner because you feel like your spouse isn't cooperating or you can't afford to do it right now. I've heard people say, "She understands" or, "This is the sacrifice we must make in order to get what we want." If your marriage is not a priority, something else will be. Extended time devoted to other things and other people compromises the intimacy and stability in your marriage. When those are compromised, the relationship suffers.

My suggestion is a vacation of some sort for just the two of you. Extended time is best, but if money, childcare, or time off are issues, a getaway weekend can do the trick. The key is only the two of you can attend.

One of the ground rules must be that there will be absolutely no arguing during this time. The purpose is to fall in love all over again, so whatever it takes for that to happen, get to it. Also, very few distractions are allowed. Limit the time checking emails or tweeting and Facebooking, unless of course you're sharing admiring updates about the awesomeness of your mate.

My husband and I have made a habit of taking one vacation with our children and one without. This has worked in our favor because we have family and friends close to home who can care for our children. This may not be an option for you. If that is the case, think of some destinations that include childcare. A cruise is great because it offers the best of both worlds. You get extended periods of time when the children can be cared for by the cruise staff, and then you have family time together.

I know a cruise sounds like a great expense, but it can be paid for in increments and represents a great value since all meals are included. The Bible states that where your heart is, there your treasure will be also (see Matthew 6:21), so put some money behind the love you claim to have. The time you spend away from one another erodes the fabric of your healthy marriage, so be intentional about restoring and rejuvenating the love you share. At the same time, a marriage revival may be nothing more than sitting in a hotel room for a day or two, just getting to know one another all over again. If you can't afford a hotel stay, empty the house of all children and make your bedroom a marital oasis for a night or two. Clean it like a maid would and do everything you would do in a hotel room — and

MARRIAGE CHALLENGES

I mean everything.

During our revival times together, we indulge in things we might not do on a regular basis. We might have an extravagant dining experience, or go to a jazz club, or just about anything that might pique our interest. A money-saving idea is a dollar movie or a home-cooked meal that you can prepare together. We have even found enjoyment in a drive to a nearby park and just sitting and laughing about memories we've created.

Our vacations have served as our marriage revivals, so whether you vacay or stay-cay, make it your goal to enjoy a time of coming together and refreshing in order to find a renewed sense of purpose, inspiration, and motivation for your marriage.

THE CHALLENGE

This week's challenge is to actually work at reviving that marriage. Although this activity may not take place this week, the goal is to plan it this week. Plan a week-long cruise, vacation away, or a weekend trip to a cabin in the woods. This is a trip for only the two of you. Plan to take part in some activity you truly enjoy, but I double dog dare you to plan to do something neither of you have tried. This creates memories only the two of you share.

If money is at issue, then plan that stay-cation. Make an area of your house look like a hotel by cleaning it, decorating it, and even placing a chocolate or towel animal on the pillow. The most important thing is to get rid of all distractions. Try to send the kids to the grandparents, the dog to a dog sitter, and leave the laundry and other chores for when your "trip" is over. Plan to spend as much time as possible enjoying one another and reviving the relationship you once had.

VERSE TO REMEMBER

"Nevertheless let every one of you in particular so love his wife even as himself; and the wife see that she reverences her husband" (Ephesians 5:33, KJV).

WEEK FIFTY
HAPPY HUSBAND'S DAY

In the last twenty-eight years, my husband and I have gone through a lot of changes. We've grown from love sick (and somewhat toxic) teenagers into middle-aged adults navigating love and life together. During this time, I often forget the fact that this man has stood by me through it all. When we found out we would be teenaged parents, he was there. When we did this again because we didn't learn from the first time, he was there. When I had to fight through the demons of sexual abuse, he was there. When our children took their first steps, lost their first tooth, and needed a shoulder to cry on, he was there. When I graduated from both high school and college, he was there. When I needed surgery, hospitalization, or simply needed a Band-Aid, he was there.

I could go on and on about the wonderful things he has done, the wonderful experiences we've had, and the wonderful memories we've made. The problem is I can easily share them with you and neglect to share them with my husband.

If you've been paying attention up to this point in the book, you know my husband has a tendency to get on my last nerve. He is a man and I am a woman, and that fact alone makes us polar oppo-

MARRIAGE CHALLENGES

sites on most subjects. When you hear the term "opposites attract," you should see our faces, because we are definitely night and day. If you've been reading carefully, you should have picked up on the fact that despite all of our differences and difficulties, he is the love of my life and I wouldn't trade him for the world.

As we traversed through yet another difficult familial situation, I came to realize this man is truly my rock. He is hurting and feeling the pain as I am, but continues to make sure I'm okay. He rubs my shoulders, holds me, and says the things I need to hear in order to get through this as we have gotten through everything else. I also realize I may not show him how much I truly appreciate all he does.

My goal in this somewhat lengthy chapter is to let everyone know that "Husband's Day" is now part of my official holiday calendar. I realize Father's Day comes up every June, but this is something completely separate. Although we give one another gifts on both Mother's and Father's Day, we've always questioned it, because he's not my father and I doggone sure am not his mother. Husband's Day allows me to give him a special shout out for all he is to me.

With that announcement ladies, take some time to first think about all your husband does for you and with you in mind. Think about what his love and relationship mean to you. Then prepare a wonderful "thank you" day to show him just how much you appreciate him. Men: Wife's Day is on the horizon (get ready for it)!

THE CHALLENGE

The goal for this week is to tell your spouse every positive thing you can think of about him or her. Find a special way to celebrate your spouse. Shout it from the rooftops, post it on social media, and let the world know how special this person is.

VERSE TO REMEMBER

"Wives submit yourselves unto your own husbands as it is fit in the Lord" (Colossians 3:18, KJV).

WEEK FIFTY-ONE
TEMPTATION

My daughter and I were having a conversation about the movie *Temptation*. There's a specific line where the wife says, "My husband forgot my birthday."

This can be a very painful situation. My daughter asked me what I would do if my husband forgot my birthday. I started to question how that's even possible. I should add that this hasn't happened yet so I can't say I know from experience, but I believe at this point it wouldn't matter. I know we all want to believe we would exercise more grace in a situation we aren't yet in. I do, however, believe I would be okay if my husband forgot my birthday.

The reality is my husband treats me like a queen on most days. He tries to make me feel special regularly. He works at this marriage thing. Does he always get it right? Oh no, but he works at it.

We do things like date nights, talk nights, and days where we just drive by ourselves with no real purpose or destination. This may seem crazy with gas at $3.00 per gallon, but it serves our marriage so well.

Be purposeful in giving one another undivided attention. Be purposeful in seeing your mate as the most beautiful person in the world. Allow your spouse to catch you checking him or her out often. Compliment your spouse regularly, but also to his or her friends and family. Don't do this with a manipulative, self-serving motive, but simply because you love and admire him or her and you want everyone to know it (hopefully they will share your words with your spouse, which is an added bonus).

A school administrator I worked with receives a pick up line via text from her husband every day. They are so corny that it makes her laugh out loud in the middle of corporate meetings and professional settings. This may seem completely inappropriate to some, but it seals their marriage for the long haul.

Being purposeful about making your spouse happy is yet another great way to make the magic last. Who can argue with someone who works at making their day special every day, even if that just means making the coffee, or starting the car? My husband gets up and shovels snow before I go to work. This wouldn't mean so much except that he doesn't even have to get out of bed until at least two hours after me. He makes the extra effort to get up and go out in the cold to ensure everything is clear for me. That blesses me beyond belief. I don't think I've ever even told him how grateful I am for that, but he does it without ever receiving a pat on the back or a thank you. That to me is love.

Now what can you do to block temptation and to make your spouse so happy that he/she doesn't even care if you forget their birthday? Work at making your spouse happy, because a happy marriage is better than having a birthday every day.

Remember:

"The marriage that laughs is the marriage that lasts"
- Fabyonne Williams.

"A successful marriage requires falling in love many times, always with the same person" - Mignon McLaughlin.

"It is not a lack of love but a lack of friendship that makes unhappy marriages" - Nietzsche.

"Happily ever after is not a fairy tale, it's a choice" - Fawn

Weaver.

"A happy marriage is the union of two good forgivers" - Ruth Bell Graham.

"To find someone who will love you for no reason, and to shower that person with reasons, that is the ultimate happiness" - Robert Brault.

And last but not least:

"Where there is love there is life" - Gandhi.

Give life to your spouse by showering him or her with love on a daily basis.

THE CHALLENGE

Do something completely out of the ordinary this week. Plan a trip to nowhere or an activity you may have never tried before. Some new things I would love to try would include zip lining, horseback riding, body painting, belly dancing, or any other activity that is out of the ordinary for you. Make your marriage a place filled with love, laughs, and adventure. Keep it interesting and fresh by making new memories together.

VERSE TO REMEMBER

"Dear friends let us continue to love one another, for love comes from God. Anyone who loves is a child of God and knows God" (1 John 4:7, NIV).

WEEK FIFTY-TWO
SHE REALLY LOVES HIM

I recently had an epiphany that took me by surprise. My son was leaving for the Air Force's basic training and we went to a bowling party planned by his beautiful wife. She did everything, but I was ill and wasn't able to enjoy it all. She tries to be upbeat and bubbly all of the time, but today she just wasn't herself. In the midst of all the fun and activity, there was a moment when I caught her standing alone and staring at him across the bowling alley. It was at that moment I realized, "She loves him as much as I do."

Anyone who knows my daughter-in-law knows she is a bundle of energy, a little ball of fire that can't be extinguished. To see her pause in the midst of all of this excitement was God's way of showing me the blessing my son has been given. She stopped and stared, and the permanent smile on her face disappeared for a moment. Then I was able to see the pain, fear, and sadness she was experiencing in saying goodbye to the love of her life. My epiphany was this: *My* son is the love of her life, and my son is also one of the three precious gifts that I love so dearly.

It opened my eyes to the reason some mothers-in-law are angry and bitter, so much so that they give their children a hard time when it comes to marriage. They aren't willing to let go of their children. This could simply be selfishness on their part or because their child has chosen some crazy babe or man who Mamma can see right through. I took a few seconds to thank God for allowing me to experience this moment with her (and she doesn't even know I had it). He allowed me to travel back to the days when I had to watch my husband travel off to wherever for whatever reason and it tore my heart out. It caused me to remember how much greater our reunions were because of the distance between us during his time away. It also reminded me that God blessed me with a daughter-in-love and not a daughter-in-law, and I am forever grateful.

I pray God sustains their marriage in this time apart and grows them even closer together. I also pray that He uses this time to pour into each one of them separately so they come back together and be that much stronger.

THE CHALLENGE

Today's challenge is once again a little different. The objective is to love on your in-laws, whether mother-, father-, son-, or daughter-in-law. I know for some this may be difficult, but it is important to your marriage. Spend the week documenting some of the reasons you are grateful for your in-laws. Use this information to write them a letter, send a card, or have a conversation about how grateful you are for them and any situation, trait, or incident that involves them and is memorable. Be sure to keep it positive. If for whatever reason your relationship with your in-laws is not the greatest, you may at least be able to thank them for raising your spouse, for babysitting, or anything else you can think of. The goal is to go deeper than this, but let's take baby steps.

When you and your spouse come together, talk about this activity. Talk about the in-law's reactions and how it made you feel. Be sure to stick to the positive aspects of the situation and not focus on any negatives. This is not being fake or phony, just focusing on the good and not the bad.

MARRIAGE CHALLENGES

VERSE TO REMEMBER

"But Ruth replied, 'Don't urge me to leave you or to turn back from you [Naomi, her mother-in-law]. Where you go I will go, and where you stay I will stay. Your people will be my people and your God my God'" (Ruth 1:16, NIV).

PROLOGUE

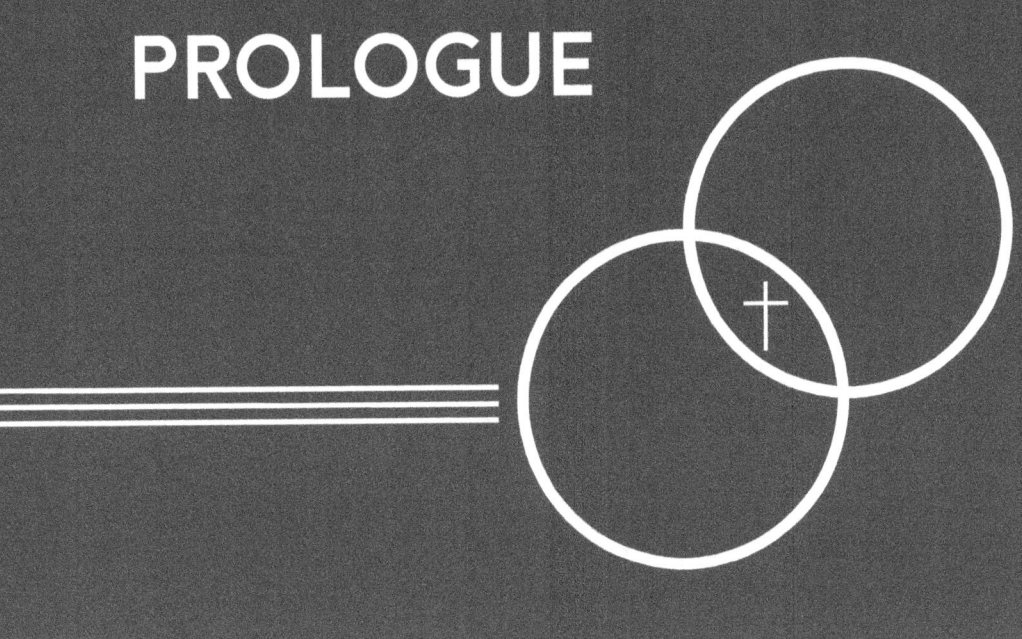

Congratulations! You have made a major deposit into the most important relationship of your life by spending a year working on your marriage together. Give yourselves a pat on the back and take a bow (or curtsy if that's more your style). I pray that God continues to bless your marriage for the diligent effort you put into making your bond a priority.

Remember to do a few things from this point on.

1. Don't let it end here! Continue your date-night routine, utilize the tools you may have put into practice to build your communication skills, and respect uninterrupted quality time for the two of you.

2. Read your journal often. You may choose a specific time to refer back to the things you wrote in your journal. Special days like anniversaries or birthdays can be good ones, or you may set aside some time on a regular basis, like for example the first Saturday of the month or every Friday night. Either way, don't allow all of this high-quality, self-reflective information to sit untouched. Use it to your advantage and to the advantage of your relationship.

3. Pay it forward! Share this experience with as many couples

MARRIAGE CHALLENGES

as you can. Remember that the divorce rate is close to if not exceeding 50%, and couples who look like everything is wonderful could be dying inside. Sharing your experience could be talking about it to the couples you know, blessing a couple or two with a copy of the book, or even facilitating a couples book club or small group and walking through it together for a year. Whatever sharing looks like for you, just make it your charge to bless as many couples as possible with the experience you and your spouse just shared.

4. Finally, refer to the book often. You may want to revise an activity or complete one you had to skip for whatever reason. You may want to do a revised version of 20 Questions or play *Make Me Laugh* one more time. You may even want to take the challenge again every couple of years just to fall in love over and over again. Whatever you do, don't allow this momentum to end. You are involved in the work of building a great relationship, so keep up the good work.

I would love to hear from you about how these challenges helped you in your marriage. Please feel free to email me at:

fabyonne@hotmail.com

APPENDIX ONE
ENCOURAGING BIBLE PASSAGES

Here are some passages you may wish to refer to when times get tough, so that you can stay encouraged. Remember, what you are going through will pass one day.

"Peace I leave with you; my peace I give to you; not as the world gives do I give to you. Let not your heart be troubled, neither let it be afraid" (John 14:27, NKJV).

"God is our refuge and strength, a very present help in trouble. Therefore, we will not fear" (Psalm 46:1-2a, NKJV).

"As for me, I will call upon God, and the Lord shall save me. Evening and morning and at noon, I will pray, and cry aloud, and He shall hear my voice" (Psalm 55:16-17, NKJV)

"He who dwells in the secret place of the Most High, shall abide under the shadow of the Almighty. I will say of the Lord, "He is my refuge and my fortress; My God, in Him I will trust" (Psalm 91:1-2, NKJ).

MARRIAGE CHALLENGES

"Therefore humble yourselves under the mighty hand of God, that He may exalt you in due time, casting all your care upon Him, for He cares for you"
(1 Peter 5:6-7, NKJV).

"Be anxious for nothing, but in everything by prayer and supplication, with thanksgiving, let your requests be made known to God; and the peace of God, which surpasses all understanding, will guard your hearts and minds through Christ Jesus"
(Philippians 4:6-7, NKJV).

APPENDIX TWO
MONTH-BY-MONTH DATING IDEAS

January

week 1 — **Go to a museum.** This should preferably be somewhere neither of you have been so it's a new experience you can share. Explore everything about the museum together and remember to take pictures in order to hold on to the memory. Find something inspiring, funny, or entertaining, and be sure to have a conversation about it. Upon completion of the museum trip, eat food (Sorry, I'm an *Elf* fan).

week 2 — **Have dinner and take in a movie.** In much of the nation, it's winter and gets dark early. Inside fun is a great way to spend a date night. Take time to find a movie you will both enjoy. It may end up being an old film festival at an artsy theater instead of the regular movie theater, but do your research and make sure both will be pleased. This can also be done in the comfort of your own home.

week 3 — **Dance class.** Take a dance class and dance the night away. Many clubs and community colleges offer a series of classes for a small fee, so this could become a month-long, date night experience if you sign up.

week 4   **Go to a comedy club.** Nothing bonds a couple more than a good hearty gut laugh. Take the time to find a good comedy club in your area, or research some comedy shows that are close enough for you and your spouse to get to. Perhaps you can rent a comedy show on Netflix or purchase a DVD presentation of your favorite comedian.

February

week 1   **Read a book together.** This could consist of either reading the book aloud together, or reading a chapter at a time and talking about it. This isn't the time to pick a 500-page novel, but a 100-page or less quick read may be a doable option for a date night.

week 2   **Go roller skating.** This can be fun for the entire family. Yes, a couple's night is necessary but childcare can also become extremely pricey. A family date night can be great as long as it doesn't always take the place of the two of you spending time alone.

week 3   **Attend a sports event.** Attend a sporting event the two of you can enjoy. This can be major or minor league performers, but the key is the two of you being together. If you aren't the sports type and your spouse is, this may be the time to compromise and splurge on some $20 nachos while you endure the experience.

week 4   **Pottery making.** Never underestimate the power of building something together. I have to be honest here. This is where our competitive natures would come out, and I'm sure we would spend the day trying to finish the project first or have the larger work of art, but that summarizes our relationship in a nutshell. It is much more fulfilling to create something together and display it somewhere in your home to remind you of the wonderful evening you had together.

March

week 1   **Dancing.** Many restaurants have dance floors. Find one that the two of you may enjoy and test it out. Enjoy a wonderful meal and then dance the night away. You may even test out the dance moves you learned when you went to dance class.

week 2   **Work out together.** This could include a trip to the gym where you go from machine to machine with one another, or a formal class in which the two of you can participate. Honestly, you could even stay home and pop in a workout video and struggle through it together. It is often fun to watch or to be watched having a difficult time with the program.

week 3   **Massage.** Follow up workout day with a date to a spa. There are many spas that offer great deals for first-time customers. The best experience Shel and I actually had was when we sprung for a couple's massage. We were massaged side-by-side in a romantic room. We had soft music playing and at the end they put our hands together. It doesn't have to be this involved but make it a great experience.

week 4   **Attend a car/RV/home show.** These can be great because they are packed with people, there's usually food, and new, hot stuff everywhere. Take a walk through a new RV or sit in the new prototype of a future car. Overall, just have a good time exploring, knowing you are creating memories that you may soon see on the roads around you.

April

week 1   **Attend a play.** This can be a professional or a less-than-professional play, but attend together and enjoy the evening.

MARRIAGE CHALLENGES

week 2 **Brunch date.** Rather than going to a restaurant in the area, take a mini road trip to a restaurant for brunch that's an hour or two from where you live. This allows you to have talk time in the car, enjoy a good meal, and then have a fun ride home. It takes on the feel of a vacation without the expense of accommodations.

week 3 **Jazz club.** Attend a club or restaurant with live entertainment. Sit side-by-side so you can touch one another because often the music is too loud to allow for conversation. If there is a dance floor, you may take some time to dance and enjoy yourselves, but if you don't do that, just bop back and forth in your seats to the sounds of music you love together.

week 4 **Bowling night.** This may be fun to do with friends. The most important part of inviting friends on a date night is that they must be positive. After your week of working and running around, this is sacred time to enjoy with your spouse. If you are going to invite anyone into this space, you cannot allow them to steal the joy you have with one another.

May

week 1 **Gallery crawl.** Many areas have tours of the different artistic venues in order to introduce locals to treasures they may not be aware are right around them. Take part and possibly get to know your neighbors as you become familiar with the galleries around you.

week 2 **Boxing.** This could get dangerous. Be sure to never, ever do this after an argument. This is a great form of exercise, however, and can be a lot of fun.

week 3 **Take in a cultural experience.** Find an opera, a ballet, or some other cultural experience you might not normally attend. If this is already your norm, then change it up; attend a non-musical theater show or something else that is outside of what you regularly enjoy. Whether you like it or not, you can put a definitive answer to why you like or don't like that experience, while you get to spend more time together.

week 4   **Street fair.** Many areas have street fairs and festivals. Research some of the more popular ones, and spend a day together browsing and enjoying the vendors, food, and shows.

June

week 1   **Canoeing.** If you live near water, most waterfront areas have rentals of canoes that are very inexpensive. Rent a canoe and spend the day paddling on the water. If you don't live near water, and there is water close enough to make a nice day trip to, why not make it a unique experience?

week 2   **Go to an amusement park.** Scream your heads off and act like kids.

week 3   **Bike riding.** This is a great form of exercise and it can be fun. Find a safe trail and ride the day away.

week 4   **City tour.** Most cities offer some type of city tour to introduce locals to what's in the area. There are walking tours, but for this date, find some type of vehicle. This could be a Just Ducky tour like they have in many cities with bodies of water, a double-decker bus, or a horse and buggy. Just find some different way to tour the city, preferably with a tour guide. Hold on to at least one piece of information you learn from the tour to share with friends. This knowledge will impress others and remind you of your special day.

July

week 1   **The zoo.** Animals make great conversation pieces for a date. Spend the day at the zoo acting silly and joking about the antics of the animals. The Pittsburgh Zoo even has a behind-the-scenes tour where you can spend time petting the animals while learning about some of the animals. This is a great experience to share with your spouse.

week 2   **A boat ride.** There's something about being on water that immediately breeds romance. Whether you do a pontoon, rent a speed boat, or get on a larger boat to share with others, enjoy the ride and make it as romantic as possible.

week 3   **Drive-in movies.** If your area no longer has a drive-in movie theater, take a portable DVD player or a computer out to the car and make a night of it. Otherwise set up shop in your car at the drive-in and have a great time. We often take a bag of snacks and, depending on which theater we go to, we grab a pizza or some other food that will hold.

week 4   **Take a vacation.** If possible, make it just the two of you, and even if it's only an overnight trip, have the time of your lives. Plan every detail from where you'll eat to what you'll do. This could be anything from walking through a special park, boardwalk, or city attraction, to never leaving the room (wink, wink). If alone is not an option, find somewhere with activities to occupy kids so you can get some alone time. Most resorts have some type of childcare or camp activities.

August

week 1   **Rent a Segway.** Many cities now teach you how to ride a Segway, and then allow you to rent one for a certain time period. Rent a Segway and have a ball.

week 2   **Skydiving.** I realize this is not for everyone and it can get pretty expensive, but the key to this date is to do something daring together. This could be bungee jumping, rock climbing, aerial yoga, or eating the atomic wings at Quaker Steak. It will create a memory that lasts a lifetime and at Quaker Steak, your names will be on the wall for at least one year.

week 3   **A scenic walk.** Walking, talking, and holding hands allows you to pour into one another as you slow down to take time and smell the roses. This walk could be to a mountain peak, or through the largest area park. Waterfalls are nice and romantic, and so are expansive views. Consider taking a basket with you or just something you can eat when you get to a somewhat secluded yet beautiful point along your walk.

week 4   **Cooking class.** Get your creative juices flowing as you attend a class and create culinary masterpieces together. The greatest part of this date is you get to eat all of your art.

September

week 1   **Blind date.** Although you know one another, who says you can't surprise your spouse with a date night he or she knows nothing about. Plan everything from the clothing to the venue. Make it interesting and an evening neither of you will ever forget.

week 2   **Food-tasting tour.** Spend the evening or day together walking a heavily-populated area rich with restaurants. Go from restaurant to restaurant, either asking for samples or testing a small item on their menu. Sharing is romantic and leaves you with more money to use at each venue. This experience familiarizes you with restaurants you might not otherwise try in your area and, of course, allows you to do this together.

week 3   **Piano bars.** If karaoke is just too daring for you but you still love to sing, a piano bar may be just your thing. You get to sing along to songs you usually know at least some of the words to, and you develop a bond with those around you who can't help but belt out a verse or chorus when that special song is played.

week 4   **Go to an ethnic restaurant.** Thai, Japanese, Chinese, Mexican whatever you may like, go ahead and try one. The best way to go is somewhere that completely immerses you in the culture so you come away feeling like you had an experience as well as a date.

October

week 1   **Winery.** Whether you drink wine or not, wineries are a wonderful experience. The ultimate is a wine-tasting tour. It is interesting because it teaches you how the wine is made, allows you to tour a beautiful facility, and it's usually pretty romantic. For those of us who enjoy indulging a little, the pièce de résistance is you get to try the wine. Many wineries also have restaurants now. This allows the experience and then you get to 'eat food.' I can add I have not had a bad experience at a winery's restaurant yet.

week 2   **Home Depot.** I never imagined I'd advocate for a building supply store on a date, but hearing how many people enjoy it floored me (pardon the pun). Take a day and go to your nearest Lowe's, Home Depot, or other home improvement/builder supply store. You can dream of things you'd love to have and plan projects you may one day work on together.

week 3   **Karaoke.** I know some people cringe at the idea of karaoke. Being the audience is fun because you get to act like an *American Idol* judge, and laugh and enjoy yourself. Being the stars is also great because it turns date night into a memorable experience.

week 4   **Community education.** Community colleges usually offer courses to the general public for a small fee. These classes range from balancing a checkbook to speaking French. Taking one of these classes guarantees time together and allows you both to better yourself in that time.

November

week 1   **Dave and Busters or an arcade.** Food and fun —

FABYONNE WILLIAMS

☑ enough said.

week 2   **Do something on your bucket list.** Since the movie *Bucket List* came out, many people have written their own lists. Share your list and if you haven't written one, take some time to do that. When your lists are complete, find some things you can do together to check off one of your dreams.

week 3   **Scavenger hunt date.** This will take some planning. Plant clues and prizes all over the place. This can happen in your house or at a local mall if you can get agreement from vendors. Make your spouse do all kinds of crazy activities and document every minute of it.

week 4   **Dinner theater.** This can get a little pricey. Sheldon and I try to justify the cost by cutting it in half and seeing half for the price of the food and half for the price of the entertainment. A more economical option could be going to a semi-professional performance often offered at restaurants to draw patrons. The experience is unmatched even when the acting is bad (bad acting turns even the most dramatic script into a comedy). You get to spend the evening with the love of your life while you eat and are being entertained.

December

week 1   **Volunteer work.** Serving others not only helps the community, but it makes you feel warm and fuzzy inside. Serving others together creates a stronger bond between you. Find some volunteer opportunities that allow you to do something important. This could be anything from serving meals to cleaning up an outside area, but it serves multiple purposes of service and time together.

week 2   **Themed movie night.** Rent a movie or pull out an oldie-but-goodie from your collection, and plan an evening at home celebrating that theme. For example, if it's *Why Did I*

MARRIAGE CHALLENGES

Get Married?, make a cute little wedding cake, drink out of flutes, and eat on decorative (paper) plates (let's keep it economical). You may even want to dress up as bride and groom just to go to an extreme to be silly.

week 3 **Ice skating.** 'Tis the season for ice events. Most areas have an ice rink open to celebrate the holiday season. If you know how to ice skate, it can be fun and if you don't, falling together will be exhilarating and hilarious. Pictures are a must.

week 4 **Living-room basket.** Lay out a blanket in the living or a private space, put a basket together of some of your favorite things, and spend the evening/day acting as if you're in the middle of a park, despite the fact that it's the middle of winter.

Alternate **Game night.** Find a game the two of you love and spend the entire evening playing and having a great time together.

Alternate **Horseback riding.** There's just something romantic about horseback riding. I don't know exactly what it is, but it can often lead to an awesome time of enjoyment.

APPENDIX THREE
BUDGET SPREADSHEET
CONTRIBUTED BY JAMES SCHINDLER

Completed by _____

Date _____

You should have personal financial statements to:
Clearly understand your situation
Measure your progress
Ensure you make the right choices

Most people prepare financial statements for their:
Mortgage broker
Credit card company
Loan officer

Many people do not have a set of their own comprehensive financial statements for evaluation purposes,

After our review, you should keep these financial statements:
To assess your financial situation
To use as a reference when making financial decisions
To help you plan for your financial future

MARRIAGE CHALLENGES

To complete this overview, look for information in your:
Paper files
Computer files
Checkbook register

Some people need less than an hour to complete the Financial Overview, especially if their finances are already summarized. For others this project may take several hours.

Please complete this overview and return it to me before our next meeting. The information will save us considerable time and will provide you with valuable data to use throughout the next year. I will return your Financial Overview to you once we have completed your financial review.

If you do not have exact amounts, enter your best estimates.

Your information will be kept strictly confidential in accordance with privacy regulations.

Note: Remember to bring all important papers to the next meeting.

Income Statement

The purpose of an income statement is to summarize your sources of income. This information allows you to make informed financial decisions on matters that affect cash flow.

Monthly Income	Gross	Net
Full-time employment		
Spouse/partner full-time employment		
Part-time employment		
Spouse/partner part-time employment		
Alimony, support income		
Spouse/partner alimony, support income		
Pensions, annuity income		
Spouse/partner pension, annuity income		
Other		
Other		
TOTAL MONTHLY INCOME	$	$

FABYONNE WILLIAMS

Do you or your spouse/partner have fluctuating incomes? When and by how much? Is your work subject to seasonal changes or layoffs? When?

_____
_____
_____
_____

Are you aware of any major changes in your finances over the next year that will make a significant difference to your available cash flow?

_____
_____
_____
_____

Periodic Income

Fill in sources and projected amounts of income for the next year. Periodic income sources might include bonus income, pay increases, interest income, dividend or royalty income, monetary gifts, inheritances, net capital gains, net rental income, sale of property, income tax refunds, income from trusts or any other net investment income.

Income Source	Self	S/P	Date Expected	Amount
Total Additional Income For You				
Total Additional Income For Your Spouse/Partner				
Approximate Addional After-Tax Household Income				

Monthly Expenses

	Amount
Accommodation	$
Rent/mortgage payment	
Property Taxes	
Utilities	
Maintenance Improvements	
Telephone, Internet access, cable	
Food	$
Groceries	
Meals away from home	
Other	
Personal Expenses	$
Personal Care	
Medical, dental, health care, prescriptions	
Laundry, dry cleaning	
Clothing	
Education, memberships	
Other	
Transportation	$
Car loan, lease payments	
Maintenance, repairs, parking, registration	
Fuel expense	
Public Transportation	
Other	
Entertainment	$
Family entertainment	
Travel, vacations,	
Sports, hobbies, special interests	
Subscriptions, books	
Other	

FABYONNE WILLIAMS

Miscellaneous $

Gifts
Professional fees
Alimony, child support
Child care, babysitting
Household help
Support to an aging parent
Charitable contributions
Pet care
Other

Insurance
(Average monthly costs)

Payroll Deduction
Y   N

Personal life insurance
Disability insurance
Health insurance
Long-term care insurance
Mortgage insurance
Homeowners insurance
Automobile insurance
Liability insurance
Other insurance

Savings Allocations

Retirement/Pension Plans (Purpose)

Investment Programs

Educational Funding

Loan Payment (not already covered) & Purpose
Institution/Person

Total Monthly Expenses $ _____

Debt Reduction
Mortgages, Loans, Credit Lines

Name of Institution/Pay Off Date	Outstanding Balance	Interest Rate	Monthly Payment
			$
	$		$
	$		$
	$		$
	$		$
	$		$
	$		$
	$		$
	$		$
	$		$
TOTALS	$		$

Which of the above loans will probably be extended because of the need to upgrade?

FABYONNE WILLIAMS

Credit Cards

Name of Institution/Pay Off Date	Outstanding Balance	Interest Rate	Monthly Payment
			$
	$		$
	$		$
	$		$
	$		$
	$		$
	$		$
	$		$
	$		$
	$		$
TOTALS	$		$

Financial Objectives

How do you handle credit cards? Do you pay off complete balances each month, pay the minimum due, or do you have a special formula to use? Please describe.

In the next year, we would like to:

MARRIAGE CHALLENGES

I/We would define financial security as:

My/Our long-term financial objectives are to:

I/We want to save/invest more because:

FABYONNE WILLIAMS

Net Worth Statement

Assets

Personal Use Assets	Current Market Value
Personal Residence	
Household furnishings, appliance	
Vacation properties	
Vehicles, boats	
Items used for hobbies	
Computer, Audio-visual equipment, electronics	
Jewelry, furs, arts, antiques, valuables, collections	
Other	
Other	
Total Personal Assets	$

Investment Assets	
Savings accounts	
Certificates of deposits	
Life insurance cash values, equities	
Stocks/Mutual funds, investments	
Real Estate (excluding your principal residence)	
Business interests	
Employer retirement plans	
Tax-deferred savings	
Other	
Other	
Total Investment Assets	$
Total Personal Use and Investment Assets	$

Liabilities

Personal Liabilities	Amount Owed
Mortgages	
	$

MARRIAGE CHALLENGES

Outstanding Loans   **Amount Owed**

	$

Credit lines & other loans

	$

Credit cards

	$

Other

	$

Total Liabilities $ _____

Personal Net Worth

Total Personal Use & Investments Assets $ _____
Less: Total Liabilities $ _____
               Total Personal Net Worth $ _____

FABYONNE WILLIAMS

Estate Net Worth (for completion during the planning meeting)

Total Investment Assets	$ _____
Add: Insurance & Pension Death Benefits	_____
Equals: Total Estate Value	$ _____
Subtract: Uninsured Liabilities	_____
Life Insurance Cash Values	_____
Total Personal Net Worth	$ _____

APPENDIX FOUR
THE FEELING WHEEL
DEVELOPED BY DR. GLORIA WILCOX

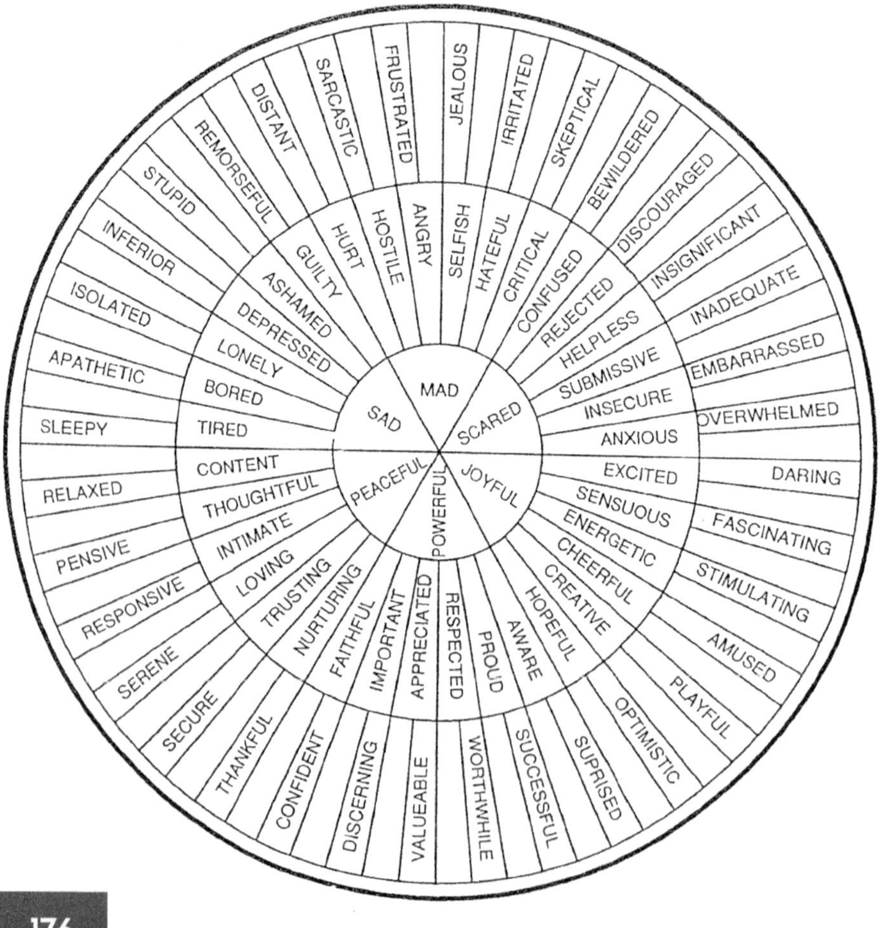

www.ingramcontent.com/pod-product-compliance
Lightning Source LLC
LaVergne TN
LVHW021559070426
835507LV00014B/1862